random moments of grace

random moments of grace

EXPERIENCING GOD *in the* ADVENTURES *of* MOTHERHOOD

GINNY KUBITZ MOYER

LOYOLAPRESS.
A JESUIT MINISTRY
Chicago

LOYOLAPRESS.
A JESUIT MINISTRY

3441 N. Ashland Avenue
Chicago, Illinois 60657
(800) 621-1008
www.loyolapress.com

Scripture quotations contained herein are from the *New Revised Standard Version Bible: Catholic Edition*, copyright © 1993 and 1989 by the Division of Christian Education of the National Council of the Churches of Christ in the U.S.A. Used by permission. All rights reserved.

A previous version of material from chapter 11 appeared as "Heart to Heart" in *U.S. Catholic*, Volume 74, No. 5 (May 2010), 47–48.

Art Credit: Nona Reina/Fotografía/Getty Images.

Library of Congress Cataloging-in-Publication Data
Moyer, Ginny Kubitz.
  Random MOMents of grace : experiencing God in the adventures of motherhood / Moyer, Ginny.
    pages cm
  ISBN-13: 978-0-8294-3840-6
  ISBN-10: 0-8294-3840-8
  1. Motherhood—Religious aspects—Christianity. 2. Mothers—Religious life. I. Title.
  BV4529.18.M69 2013
  248.8'431—dc23

                                                              2012044952

Printed in the United States of America.
13 14 15 16 17 18 Versa 10 9 8 7 6 5 4 3 2 1

For Matthew and Luke,
with love beyond all telling

Contents

Introduction

The Ultimate Spiritual Workout

Before I had kids, I spent lots of time nurturing my spiritual life. When I got together with friends over brunch or late-night bottles of cabernet, we'd have leisurely conversations about God and faith. Late afternoons would sometimes find me slipping into a nearly empty church, settling into a pew, and meditating in silence. A perfect weekend was one spent at a retreat house in a redwood forest or nestled among oak-studded hillsides, wandering down quiet paths and letting my thoughts unspool at their own pace. It's easy to have spiritual epiphanies when there is no sound around you but the rustle of leaves in the breeze, when you don't have to be present to anyone but yourself and God.

Things are a wee bit different now.

It would be easy to moan about what I've lost in the five years since I became a mother, namely time, space, and the ability to spend thirty seconds in the bathroom without a small boy banging on the door and asking what I'm doing. Spiritual junkie that I am, it's easy to get nostalgic for the wide spaces of silence and solitude that used to be critical ingredients for developing my inner life. How can I maintain an active spirituality when my attempts at morning prayer are interrupted by the frantic sound track of cartoons? How can I be enriched by the Mass when I spend the homily trying to keep my two small sons from wriggling on their stomachs, sniper-like, under the kneeler?

But here's what I've learned: although silence, solitude, and homilies are all very good ways to deepen one's faith life, they aren't the only means of spiritual growth. Blowing bubbles on the front lawn, fastening a child's bike helmet, and even wiping up messes can also be the raw material for a rich spiritual life. Motherhood presents you with all kinds of random moments and experiences you never could have anticipated. Some are sweet, some are transcendently beautiful, some are hilarious, and some make you want to call the nearest convent and see if it's not too late to pursue a career as a nun. But I'm learning that all of these experiences—even the deeply frustrating ones—are chances for growth and grace.

I have learned an enormous amount about sacrifice by spending an hour cleaning vomit off my son's crib (and off my son); no homily could possibly teach me more. And yet, as stinky as that hour was, it also showed me how sweet and right it feels to comfort my sick little child. I've learned that feelings of love and gratitude for my serial puker can trump even the frustration of giving him three baths in one evening. And I like to think that the whole experience edged me just a little bit closer to understanding the reality of divine love, the love that gives and then gives some more, the love that underpins the universe.

This book is a candid look at these random moments of grace and a reflection on how they have enriched my spiritual life. That's not to say that this process is easy or obvious or, for that matter, immediate. When I'm breaking up a heated fight over the remote-control Buzz Lightyear toy, I am not exactly thinking about all the rich spiritual wisdom I'm accruing from the experience. Mostly, I'm wondering if there is such a thing as a yearlong sabbatical from motherhood, and if so, where do I apply? The insights come later, during a moment of silent prayer or while I'm commuting to work or taking a shower or scribbling in a notebook. I think the key lies in approaching those chaotic moments of motherhood with a reflective frame of mind, which, frankly, is a lot harder than it sounds. But, as I tell my older son about his swimming lessons, you can't become good at something if you don't practice. That's as true of faith as it is of anything else. The ability to find God everywhere, even in places like toy-strewn living rooms, is a spiritual muscle that has been a bit flabby up until now. But motherhood gives me numerous chances to flex it, and I'm getting more buff all the time.

It's worth mentioning up front that motherhood and writing are not my only jobs. I also work outside the home, teaching high school English. I'm not sure if that makes my life easier or harder. On the upside, it gets me out of the house most days and guarantees that I will have at least some adult conversation, which is a thing you don't realize how much you need until you don't have it anymore. On the downside, working outside the home means that I'm spinning a lot of plates, and it is exhausting having to constantly anticipate and prevent a crash. (I breathe far more easily during summer vacation, a time when a few of those plates are stacked and put away.) I mention this because the amount of time you spend with your kids may be more or less than I spend with mine. Either way, I hope you still find an echo of your parenting experiences in the chapters that follow.

In the interest of full disclosure, I should also add that I fail at mindfulness about as often as I succeed. One of the challenges of writing about spirituality and motherhood is that moments after you pen a blog post or chapter that makes you sound very wise and balanced, you find your children jumping from chair to chair in the manner of penguins leaping onto Arctic ice floes, and you respond in a manner that is anything but wise and balanced. It is extremely humbling and can make you momentarily wonder if you have any business telling anyone anything about motherhood and faith.

But the reality is that I learn the most from spiritual writers and teachers who are willing to admit that they don't have it all together. If a writer comes across as too smoothly perfect, I feel as though she could never relate to raggedy-edged, imperfect me. (I also wonder what, exactly, she's hiding.) So in this book, I will try to keep it real, not ideal, acknowledging that yes, I do occasionally drop four-letter words when I step on a plastic dinosaur in my bare feet. And, yes, I believe that God is present in that moment, too.

If I've learned anything over the past five years, it's that parenthood really is the ultimate spiritual workout. There is grace to be found in every skinned knee, in every sleepless night, and in every guileless baby smile. And though I still think fondly of the days when I savored those wide watercolor spaces of peaceful solitude, the truth is that these random moments of parenting can be our best spiritual teachers, if we train our souls to listen.

1

Innocence

Why I Edit Out the Scary Stuff

One afternoon when Matthew was three and Luke was one, we were taking a bike ride around the neighborhood. Matthew was on his red Radio Flyer trike, the one with streamers hanging down from the handlebars and a little bell that chimes softly every time he crosses an uneven place in the sidewalk. I was following a few paces behind while pushing Luke, who was sitting in his stroller, chomping on Goldfish Crackers and checking out the scenery as we trundled along.

About halfway down the block, Matthew slowed and almost stopped. I could see him looking down cautiously at something on the sidewalk.

"Mommy," he called behind him, "what is that?"

I knew it couldn't be good. From where I was, I could just make out a tiny blob, pinkish, inches from the curb. A small bird? A rodent of youthful age? Antiseptic Mom surged to the fore. "I don't know, honey," I told him, "but let's not touch it. Let's just look at it and not touch it."

So Matthew, obviously intrigued and a bit concerned, wheeled slowly around the mystery object, eyes on it the whole time. As Luke and I drew nearer, I saw that it was indeed a fledgling that had fallen out of a nest, clearly from the huge trees above us. It had a gummy-looking, pale-pink body, with the occasional small patch of gray down. Even in my cursory glance, I saw its lids stretched closed over tiny eyeballs, which bulged underneath like hard little marbles. I saw the folded bony wings and the pitiful frailty of this tiny creature that had met a premature end on hard concrete.

"Let's just walk by and not touch it," I said again to Matthew, who was wheeling slowly by, still staring.

"Yes," said Matthew seriously, starting to resume speed. "It might bite us."

There are some things your kids say that just pierce you through the heart. That was one of them. Oh boy, the bird wouldn't be biting anything ever; that would have been patently clear to any adult, even to any child older than Matthew. But to him, it was just an unusual creature, something different, perhaps something dangerous. I wasn't about to correct him, to tell him that the bird posed no threat, because then I'd have to take him into some new, even more frightening territory. I'd have to talk to him about death.

I've tried to avoid the topic of death when talking with Matthew; I really have. To be honest, I'm scared to go there. What do you say to a very young child? How do you let him into that reality, the finality of it all? Can he even comprehend it at such a young age? I'm inclined to think that he can't. Actually, that's not true. I believe that he *can* grasp the idea of death, the terrifying reality of someone being gone forever from this earth. I think that he *can* understand it, and that's exactly why I want to shield him from it.

All this avoidance has led to some rather creative editing on my part. In Matthew's bedroom library is a picture book for older kids, Tomie dePaola's *The Clown of God*. It was given to me as a gift when Matthew was two, and I put it in his bookshelf, thinking it would just stay there undisturbed until he was seven or eight. Of course, Matthew promptly discovered it and requested that I read it, so it has become a part of our bedtime canon. The book is a beautifully illustrated retelling of a medieval legend about an old juggler who juggles before the statue of Mary and Jesus to offer them a gift. Just as the balls are flying in the air, the juggler's heart stops, and he slumps to the ground, dead. (There is a happy little ending a page or two later, trust me, but I don't want to spoil it here.) Suffice it to say, when I read the story, I take a few liberties with the conclusion. The juggler falls to the ground, and that is it. He just falls and lies there, resting.

Yes, I am a coward.

Actually, this is really not about being a wuss. My editing comes from a positive impulse—the desire to preserve something lovely and fragile in my kids. I want them to keep that fundamental innocence they now possess. I want them to have no reason to believe that the world is full of things such as dead birds, or jugglers who never rise again, or mean people, or crime. And I can do this only because my boys are still so young. There comes a time in kids' lives—and it's coming soon, I know it is—when you have to let them in on the darkness, if only to keep them safe. And at some point there will be people close to them who die, who just aren't there anymore. The innocence will begin to give way to knowledge, as it must do.

But oh, that innocence, it's heartbreakingly beautiful. It's not just a lack of knowledge about death and bad people but something even larger. It's the unself-conscious honesty that little kids have. It's that total trust that Mommy or Daddy can make the monsters in the closet go away. It's the pure unfiltered joy in their responses to the world, with no awareness of how they are "supposed" to behave. And I know that it's temporary. I know that Matthew won't always hug his Tigger doll and say, "He's my friend." I know that Luke won't always look at a bubble floating on the air and break into a toothy grin and a squeal of wonder, as if he's seeing the second coming of Christ. It's hard, so hard, to imagine them losing that. I hoard the beauty of their sweet innocence; I push it into the corner of my cheek like candy. But it will dissolve someday. I hope and pray that it won't happen through some huge tragedy. All I can hope is that it will be a slow, gradual, and almost imperceptible process, the inevitable reality of growing up.

As much as I want to keep their young sweetness under glass, preserved forever in some bell jar, that's not how the world works. Nothing can grow if it's being preserved. And I want my boys to grow.

All of this makes me think of Adam and Eve. Whether you take that story as literal truth or as beautiful allegory, there is something very resonant there. Two people in Paradise, with nothing wrong, no awareness that the world could ever be bad—and then, through a series of events comes the sudden consciousness of their own vulnerability. And in that moment, everything changes. There are shadows in the garden, things they suddenly need to be wary of, things they need to fear. They must always, to some extent, be on their guard. Life will never be the sweet paradise that it was before.

It's only recently that I've given any serious thought to God's reactions in this story. Yes, I've always sensed his cosmic disappointment. I've always been able to picture him as the exasperated parent who says, like the father from *The Brady Bunch*, "Kids, you'll just have to live with the consequence of your actions." But could there also have been some pain on God's part, the urge to cry at the fact that his children's innocence has gone? Maybe God also looked at them with profound sorrow, wishing like crazy that there were some way their innocence could have been preserved forever. But that is not how life is. For whatever reason, we all have to grow into the realization that there are not only roses in the garden but also rot.

We parents go to great lengths to preserve it—this beautiful innocence—and we do what we can for as long as we can. At some point, though, there's the crack in the wall, the snag in the fabric, and our children start to realize that bad things happen. And when that time comes, what can a parent do? I guess we just listen to our kids and talk to them. We hug them and try to keep certain zones there for them, safe ones we can control, a little sliver of their lives in which they know that nothing will harm them.

There is not much more we can do, really, other than savor the innocence while we have it. Matthew rattles along on his trike, and I follow behind, watching the sun glint off his Toy Story helmet, watching his little legs go up and down purposefully, and I consciously register it as a graced moment. I take a mental snapshot of it to file away for later. Or I blow bubbles for Luke on the lawn on a warm spring evening. They float through the windless air and settle on the grass, and he crawls over to them excitedly and touches them, and they pop. "Yay, Luke! You got it!" I tell him, clapping. He looks at me in surprise, and I suddenly wonder at my own reaction, why I'm applauding at the fact that something so fragile and beautiful has vanished forever.

2

Talking to God

Praying as I Can, Not as I Can't

t's 8:15 p.m. Matthew is at last in bed, his blankie tucked under his arm, his sleepered body curled up like a comma. Luke has been in his crib for half an hour already, quiet in his own darkened room.

I head for the sofa. For the first time all day, I can lie down without having to be on guard against an exuberant boy launching himself onto my stomach. Stretching out my legs, I claim as much space as I can, ignoring the Mr. Potato Head body parts strewn all over the floor like a massacre in plastic. It's evening, and the house is finally quiet; I have better things to do than pick up mustaches.

Cracking open a book of meditations, I take a deep centering breath and begin to read. After the breakneck speed of a day of teaching and parenting, the silence is golden, the solitude rare and precious. I'm focused and peaceful and ready to commune with the divine.

The next thing I know, I'm pulling up my head with a jerk. I blink at the line of text in front of me, my vision fuzzy, until I realize that I've read it before—more than once, in fact. Each time, the words have entered my brain but completely bypassed my memory, marching briskly out some side exit without leaving a trace. I find this disconcerting.

I do not, however, find it surprising. Frankly, I'm so chronically exhausted that any period of time in a reclining position inevitably leads to sleep. I actually look forward to going to the dentist, because I see it as an opportunity to catch some R & R. (Forty-five minutes of lying back in a chair? It's like a spa treatment.) I'd never have thought it possible before becoming a mom, but these days I can flirt with sleep even while getting my eyebrows waxed. It's crazy to think I can stay awake during a meditation session on the sofa, no matter how much I want to.

"You know, sleep is a form of prayer," said my husband, Scott, one evening, after just such a failed attempt. I don't know whether he was being serious or just wanted to make me feel better. And while I agree that drifting into the sweet unconsciousness of sleep can be spiritually renewing, it is not the sort of prayer I want. It's certainly not the sort of prayer I used to do.

It is not the sort of prayer I miss.

Even before having kids, I was never someone with a structured prayer routine. I nearly always did evening prayers before sleep, but I never had a morning psalm reading over coffee or a nightly meditation ritual as some of my friends did.

But though the schedule was inconsistent, the prayer itself was intense. When the desire to pray came upon me, I'd seize it. I'd sit down with a Bible or a book of reflections, settling into the easy chair or a backyard patio seat, and I'd read slowly, letting the words sink into me, answering questions I didn't always know I had. Half an hour later, I'd get up from that chair feeling wiser and more balanced, renewed by some little epiphany about the nature of God or the state of my life.

Back in the day, I also loved going to empty churches and praying quietly, savoring the coolness of the vast space around me. I would listen to the creak of the building and the rush of breezes outside the window. I'd hear the occasional dramatic boom of a kneeler being put back into place by a departing fellow pray-er, and in those spaces it was easy to feel an odd mix of restlessness and peace. The space felt alive; even when there was no one else in the church, I knew I was not alone. In those echoing empty pews, I felt the presence of God in a way that seemed vivid, even mystical.

It's hard to have that experience when there is a toddler in there with you, shooting metal cars like cue balls along the pew.

So for the first few years of my life as a mom, I more or less threw in the towel when it came to formal prayer. I got by on something else, something a spiritual director once called "opportunistic spirituality." At random moments throughout the day, I'd take a moment to ping God a little message. *Hey there. How are you? I'm here, doing fine. Just saying Hi.* That was about the sum of it: a quick check-in, a spiritual text message to the Creator. And I found that there was something freeing about this kind of prayer. I could do it anytime, anywhere—while changing a noxious diaper, driving to work, or shaving my legs. There was nothing dramatic about it, but it was helpful because it meant I could integrate God into my normal routine without breaking my step. Prayer became more reflexive, more instinctive, less an event than a way of being. It validated a favorite quotation of mine, from the English abbot John Chapman: "Pray as you can, not as you can't."

This new practice was nice, and it helped. I was taking quick, frequent sips at the well of prayer, instead of long slow drinks. I missed the luxurious gulps, I really did, but at least I was staying hydrated.

And then I started to feel parched again. It was around New Year's, when Matthew was three and Luke was one, that I became mildly obsessed with a certain image. I'd spent much of the holiday season listening to Hayley Westenra's version of the Joni Mitchell song "River," and every time she sang about longing to skate away down a river, some part of my soul sat up and took notice.

At random moments of the day, I found myself fantasizing about a snowy, moonlit landscape, bluish in tone. I pictured a frozen river cutting through the snow like a zigzag, and I was on it, on skates, a stocking cap flying out behind me as I whooshed along. There wasn't another person in this picture, just me with my long cap and the bare trees and the white banks. I was blissfully alone, following the curves of the river, gliding with sure strokes that I've never had in real life, right foot then left, right, left, my legs stretching, my thoughts unspooling, and peace coming at me like a river.

I couldn't shake that image from my mind, and it wasn't too hard to figure out what it meant: a desire for escape. It wasn't a Thelma-and-Louise type of thing; I loved my husband, kids, and life in general, and I had zero desire to drive off into the red rocks of the Southwest. But as I settled sibling squabbles, graded stacks of essays, folded laundry, and juggled doctor's appointments for three people, I knew what was eluding me: a sense of peace. I wanted a chance to be alone with my thoughts and let them come in a leisurely, steady flow, like the movement of a skater on an icy stretch of river. I wanted that sense of pulling into yourself that you get on a cold wintry day, and yet the corresponding sense of going out of yourself, the feeling you get when you move steadily through a new, uncharted landscape.

And I realized that in the absence of crucial elements of this scenario—namely, skates, a stocking cap, a frozen river, and the ability to stand upright on ice—I'd have to find my peace some other way.

>——<

In our bedroom is a brown desk. It was a hand-me-down from my sister, and for a while it sat in Matthew's room, serving absolutely no purpose at all (at the age of one, he wasn't doing much writing). A few years ago, Scott suggested that we move it into our bedroom for my personal use, and I received the suggestion with great rejoicing. It sits in the back corner, up against the windows, facing a large and particularly beautiful Japanese maple. Photos of the boys are arranged on the desk, along with a framed picture of Our Lady of Perpetual Help and a small statue of Mary that I bought in Lourdes. There's an engagement picture of Scott and me in Golden Gate Park, looking significantly younger. I've arranged a selection of books on the desk as well: a Bible, prayer books, a catalog from an art exhibition I saw in New York years ago, an illustrated volume of children's poetry.

This is often where I write. Increasingly, it's where I pray.

Most evenings, it takes a bit of effort for me to use the desk. Scott is in the unfortunate habit of piling his clothes over the back of the chair at night, which I can't really fault him for; the closets in our postwar house are teeny, far too small for a couple to share and stay happily married. So the ritual invariably begins with the transfer of my husband's clothes to someplace equally inconvenient, like the bed.

Once I've cleared a space, I sit down at the desk. I light a candle and stare at the flickering flame and let myself slip into another zone. The clutter of the house is all behind me, quite literally; even with the blinds drawn, I'm facing the outdoors, which is centering. And I sit on the hard wooden chair—it's nearly impossible to fall asleep there—and I pray.

Sometimes, I pray a decade or two of the rosary, which has the mental effect of scouring my mind free of the grease of the day. Other times, I take out a book of reflections and meditation prompts, and let my mind go. It skates off into various directions, set in motion by a question or quotation or topic, and I let it go. I invite God into the stillness, and for a few moments it feels holy and quiet. It's so rare to sit without some kind of screen in front of me, and every time I sit at the desk, screenless, I realize how much I am refreshed by that lack of visual stimuli.

And I'm finding that I need this little zone, this place that is dedicated to my inner life. When I'm there, it's just God and me and the white candle glowing in its glass holder, looking wintry and hot all at the same time. This prayer pause means that I'm bumping something else off my evening to-do list, but the time never feels wasted. Even if I don't get a dramatic St. Paul-type epiphany about my life, the pause is important simply because it affirms that there is an interior life that deserves my attention. I've found that although the quick-prayer-texts to God are helpful and good and help me integrate God into the very fabric of my life, they are ultimately not enough for me. I also need time dedicated to the unfurling of my thoughts and worries and fears, the slow glide into new perspective.

And though it took me a while to stumble upon the optimal conditions for post-motherhood prayer—the desk with a hard wooden chair, the clutter of the house behind me, the flickering candle before me—I'm glad I kept trying until I found what works. What happens at the prayer desk doesn't stay at the prayer desk, after all. Those quiet sessions help me recognize the grace that exists in all the frantic experiences of my life as a mom, gently training me to notice them more often, sometimes even as they're happening. Those moments at the desk help me pay more attention to the Spirit that is always there, just waiting for me to sit down and listen.

When I'm done, I blow out the candle, and the smoke curls upward. I remember reading that the smoke of incense represents the lifting of our prayer heavenward, and that image is perfectly fitting. And when I leave that chair, I feel both invigorated and relaxed, with that feeling you get when you've stretched a part of yourself that was once cramped and confined. It's not a quiet skate through a frozen landscape, but it is an escape into a peace that often eludes me in every other way. It's about making an effort to find the best time and place to pray, and it ends up feeling like absolutely no effort at all.

3
Community

No Mom Is an Island

When I was twenty-one, I had my first experience of being seriously ill. Just a few weeks after I returned home from my semester studying in Paris, I came down with mononucleosis. (While I'd love to deny any connection between the two, honesty compels me to add that a certain continental boyfriend may have had something to do with it.) I was at home for weeks, wrapped in misery and a cotton quilt. The sore throat felt as if I were swallowing razor blades, which was beyond awful, but once that passed, it was the boredom that almost killed me. In the days that I was housebound, I slept off and on, read a book on modern Germany, worked my way through several Audrey Hepburn movies, and put together a scrapbook of my time abroad. When I went to the doctor's office, I sat, frail and germy, in the backseat and gazed in wistful envy at the world scrolling by outside the car windows.

I experienced a similar feeling when Matthew was a newborn. As I recovered from my C-section, hobbling around the house, adjusting to the joys but also (let's get real) the totally overwhelming demands on my time, attention, and physical person, I once again gazed out the window like a lost soul. It was as though I'd disappeared into a vortex of parenting, one penetrated only by my husband, my mom, occasionally my dad, and Matthew. I lived for appointments with the lactation consultant and the pediatrician because it meant I could get out of the house and actually see people outside my immediate family. And when friends came by to see our little guy, bearing small blue outfits and dinners of Thai food or brisket or rotisserie chicken, I was eager to see them, ambassadors from that world out there that I hoped, one day, to re-enter.

It can be very isolating, parenthood. There's no question about it. And yet as my life as a mom ticked on, as the sheer survival mode of those first frantic weeks began to click into a routine of rather comfortable predictability and my thoughts were at liberty to go elsewhere, it became clear that this sense of being isolated was only one side of the coin. I learned that parenthood had also given me the polar opposite of isolation: a deeper, more intense identification with others than I would ever have thought possible. As I became a mom, new highways of connection were being laid over my life's landscape.

This connection shows up in lots of ways, big and small. I've never been one to strike up conversations with random people in the checkout line or at the mall, but since having kids, I do. If there's a mom there with a baby or a toddler—the age of my kids or younger—I'll often ask the child's age, and that one question can be the catalyst for a conversation that never would have happened otherwise. The other woman and I might have totally divergent views about what constitutes watchable TV or good foreign policy or appropriate dress at the workplace, but when we are both moms, there is an obvious, foolproof point of entry. For an introvert like me, it's been almost surprising to see how easily I can talk to a stranger as long as he or she happens to be toting a toddler on one hip. The world is smaller now, and that is a nice way for it to be.

Parenthood has also compelled me to do the unthinkable: ask others for help. This is not easy for me, because I have a total horror of imposing on other people. I have no problem asking my near and dear to step in when things are frantic, maybe because they are family and I figure they are beholden by the bonds of blood to take an interest in my life. When both Luke and Scott came down with a virulent stomach flu within two days of each other (during finals week, no less, the worst timing ever for an English teacher with ninety in-class essays to grade), I had no problem asking my father to enter our pestilent airspace and babysit. But if it's someone outside the family circle, I have an innate aversion to requesting help because I feel terrible making others rearrange their schedules, even slightly, on my behalf. It sounds extreme, but that philosophy is pretty much how I have operated throughout much of my life. And I may have persisted in that reticence, were it not for parenthood.

I remember a time when Scott came down with what appeared to be a mild flu. He stayed home from work for two days, figuring that some rest and relaxation would help the bug slowly fade away. Alas, rest and relaxation are wildly optimistic goals when you share an eleven-hundred-square-foot house with small children. At any rate, with my parents out of town and unable to watch the boys, I had to head to work on the third day and leave the big sick man in charge of the two little, frighteningly robust ones. With some trepidation I kissed him good-bye as he sat palely on the couch.

When I returned home at the end of my workday, the boys hailed me boisterously as I walked in the front door. They were still eating lunch and, by the look of things, had been doing so for hours. The TV was tuned to PBS Kids and, by the look of things, had been so for hours. The house was twice as trashed as usual, which is really saying something, and Scott was lying on his back on the sofa, totally immobile. I felt his forehead, which gave new meaning to the term *five-alarm*.

"Did you take your temperature?" I asked.

"No," he managed. "Maybe I should. I do feel kind of warm."

He was, as it turned out, 103.7 degrees of warm. It was the first time I'd seen anyone with a fever that high. "I'm calling the doctor," I said.

"With a fever like that, he really needs to be seen," the nurse told me over the phone. "Can you be here in half an hour?"

I relayed her words to Scott, who slowly and laboriously put on his shoes. It was obvious that he couldn't drive himself, and equally obvious that toting a two-year-old and a four-year-old to the doctor's office during what was supposed to be their nap time would qualify me as clinically insane, given that there was a nice retired lady across the street who was nearly always home in the afternoon. Under normal circumstances, my pathological politeness would have made me hesitate to pick up the phone and ask for a favor. But when the mercury rose, so did my ability to ask for help.

She answered almost immediately. "Of course I can watch the boys. I'll be right over." And she was.

We soon learned that Scott had an infection; fortunately, it cleared up with a few courses of antibiotics. "When you have a fever that high, you basically feel like you're dying," the doctor told me, and thinking back to that pale, immobile figure on the couch, I can guess he was just about right. And when I thanked my wonderful neighbor for her impromptu babysitting, she waved it off easily. "You'd do the same for me," she said, and you know what? She's right. And I'm more likely to do so now than I ever was before having kids, because now I know what it feels like to be in situations where there are several competing needs that have to be met at the same time. Those are the times when you need to call in reinforcements, when you need to take the risk of reaching out of your usual close circle of rescue workers. And odds are good that those new folks are more than ready to throw you a lifeline, just as long as you are able to get over your own silly politeness and yell for one.

The semester that I studied in Paris, 1994, was the year that the movie *Schindler's List* was released. I saw it in a small theater on an overcast Sunday afternoon. As I looked around the rows of seats, it occurred to me that I was watching the movie in the company of people who had actually lived it; the gray-haired Parisians in the audience surely remembered the World War II years and the experience of living under Nazi occupation. Watching the movie in that setting (in English, with French subtitles; I spoke French, but did not trust myself to follow a film that complex on my own) was a haunting experience. So many of the scenes were vivid and unforgettable: the Nazi officer banging on the piano as his compatriots trashed the house; the soldier putting the gun to the prisoner's head and those agonizing moments in which it just wouldn't fire; the little girl in the red coat, running through the ghetto. But more awful than all of these was the scene in the concentration camp when the children are led out to the trucks that will take them to their deaths. They walk along, singing like preschoolers heading out on a field trip, and the mothers see them and run screaming after them, because they know what is about to happen.

It's been years since I saw that movie, but I can hardly bear to remember that scene. It affected me deeply then, as a twenty-one-year-old college student, and yet there was something in my reaction that was more cerebral than anything else. Now that scene is exponentially more horrible because I can imagine myself living it. I see my own boys walking along in that straggling bunch of children, my own self in that screaming mass of agonized mothers. The mere thought of living through that experience is too hard to bear. And yet many women in the concentration camps did have to bear it. And even now, in various places all around the world, mothers are losing their babies, not to Nazi gas chambers but to other forces—poverty, slavery, genocide—that are equally brutal and implacable. I recognize that it is a happy accident that I live in a time and place where I don't need to fear those things, and my heart breaks for the moms who are not as fortunate.

But even in my own safe little world, there are moms who suffer terribly, losing their kids to war and suicide and accidents. The word *compassion* means "suffering with," and I can't think of a better way to explain what has happened to me since becoming a mom. When I hear a news story of a young soldier dying in Afghanistan or a child drowning in a swimming pool, I immediately think of their mothers, and I feel a physical pain inside at the thought of what they are feeling. I pray for strangers often these days because I want to do something, and sometimes I can't think of anything else to do except convert that compassion into prayer.

This compassion is a double-edged sword. It is painful to be this sensitive to others' tragedies, to be haunted by a story that I overhear on the radio. Sometimes I feel as though I were pure emotion covered with a very thin skin, like that pulsing soft spot on a newborn's head. It isn't easy to keep something that vulnerable protected from harm. At the same time, though, I am recognizing that this ability to suffer with others is, ultimately, a good thing.

As a Catholic, I've spent a lifetime looking at crucifixes. And one thing I've realized is that the figure of Jesus, bleeding and nearly naked, is a vivid invitation to compassion. He's such a vulnerable figure, hanging there on the cross, with scabby knees and depleted strength; when you really look at it, you can't help but be moved with pity for his suffering. That's why I've learned to see the crucifix as a reminder that my faith—that any faith—is at its finest when it enables us to relate to and enter into the pain of others. We all have our moments when life hurts like hell, when the things we are facing feel like crucifixion. And when we are hanging on the cross of our suffering, there is a unique comfort that comes from people who take the time to tell us that they have registered our pain. It's not even a question of fixing the pain; some hurts simply can't be mended. They can, however, be alleviated somewhat by the person who says, "I know you are hurting, and I want to support you however I can." There is, really, no more beautiful act of love than that.

That's why I don't mind the vulnerability I've developed as a mom, even though it is sometimes a difficult thing. I'm finding that this sensitivity can be the first step toward concrete acts of kindness, the catalyst for suspending judgment of others, the baby step into working for social justice and human rights. And even if all I can manage to do is pray for the mom who has just lost her twenty-year-old son to a motorcycle accident, I believe that those prayers still count for something. I think those prayers spin an invisible but tensile thread that pulls us all a little closer, tying together the various parts of this seemingly fragmented world and giving us the subtle assurance that we're not suffering alone.

No mom is an island, after all, even though there are times in our parenting lives when it feels that way. There are lines and highways of connection all around us, radiating out in every direction, and there's something downright holy about using them.

·

4

Covenant

Mommy Always Comes Back after Nap and Snack

When Matthew was younger, he went through a period of not wanting to go to preschool. He'd get weepy when Scott or I dropped him off and would hug the parental leg like a barnacle stuck to a rock. "I don't want to go! I want to stay with you!" he'd say with tears in his voice, and every time it would rip my heart out by the roots.

"But you'll have fun!" I'd say. "There are so many nice kids here! You can play outside on the playground!" I'd become a one-woman PR campaign for the preschool, desperately touting its extracurricular activities and robust social life.

But when a preschooler is in that kind of a missing-Mommy mind-set, you could promise him a personal audience with the Cat in the Hat, and the wails would continue unabated.

I had to come up with a mantra. "Mommy will pick you up after nap and snack," I'd say. I'd repeat that at multiple times of the day, hoping to make the comforting words stick in his head. "Mommy always comes after nap and snack," I'd tell him as the car neared the preschool, and he'd get a little light in his eyes, a slight softening of his crumpled face, and it seemed to help him. He knew what to expect; he knew that the day had a routine, regular as clockwork. And he knew that, no matter what, Mommy would come back after nap and snack.

And I always did.

Years ago, when I was engaged and planning the wedding, the enormity of what I was about to do started to sink in. *Wait a second: I am about to pledge the rest of my life to this relationship. I am about to stand up before God and the world and promise to love my husband through richer and poorer, for better and for worse, until we are parted by death.* I had no prior experience of making a promise like that. The closest I'd ever come to making a Big Life Decision was picking a college, which seemed like an enormous commitment at the age of eighteen—but we all know that you divorce a college after four years. Though I loved Scott and had no doubt that I'd chosen the right guy, the mere fact of making that epic a promise gave me pause.

"This is wild," I told a much older colleague of mine one day. "I'm really not used to this. Getting married will be the first promise I've ever made that I can't undo."

She smiled with the wisdom of several decades' more life experience. "That's even truer of parenthood," she said. "That's really something you can't undo."

And now that I have five years of parenting under my belt, I agree with her. Marriage was the first of the Very Big Covenants I've made, but parenthood is even larger and more primal. It feels at least as huge as God's covenant to Noah, or God's promises to Abraham. There is no way to undo my tacit vow to be there for my boys, to love them and care for them—not that I'd want to undo that promise. For richer and for poorer, in vomiting and in health, in times of sweet little boy hugs and of teenage surliness, I'm going to be there, on their side, caring for and about them. I may leave from time to time, to go to work or the grocery store or a girls' night out with my friends, but I will always come back. *Mommy always comes back after nap and snack.* Don't worry, my little boy. I will return.

I could sense the magnitude of this promise well before Matthew was born, which was part of the reason why I, in the very smallest and most secret chamber of my heart, was quietly terrified of taking the plunge into parenthood. And yet it's an undeniable truth that making a promise to another person can actually be liberating. In my marriage, for example, I've found that there's a paradoxical freedom in making a commitment to Scott and vice versa. I can trust that he will not reject me if I gain thirty pounds or get cancer or have a nervous breakdown. It's freeing to know that even if we disagree on something, there is the expectation that we'll work through it rather than let it drive us apart. Our marriage promise has also liberated me from wondering if I'd ever find a guy who could connect with me mind, body, and soul, which for years seemed about as likely as tracking down the yeti. And it also gives me a little hint of God's commitment to me. God is here for the long haul. God is not going anywhere, no matter how much I may change over the years.

The covenant to my kids is certainly freeing for them; they don't have to worry about whether or not they can count on Mom. And I've found that it's also freeing for me. No, I can't get a pedicure rather than pick them up from school. Scott and I are no longer able to drop everything and spend a cozy weekend at a little inn on the coast, something we didn't do very often in the pre-kid days. (If only we'd seized the opportunity while we had it!) But when I look a bit deeper at my unyielding commitment to my boys, I see all the ways in which it's good. There's a more definite shape to my days now, an accountability. I know where I'll be at 4:30 every day and what I'm going to do with my evenings.

Does that predictability feel boring sometimes? Absolutely. I'd be lying if I said that I do not have days when I long for a shake-up of the routine, for a dash of positive drama. There is not much that is emotionally stimulating about spending my evening fixing dinner and packing school lunches for the next day. On the scale of excitement, this period of my life certainly can't compare to my college semester in Paris or to the year I spent living and working there after graduation. Back then, I did not have to worry about cooking for anyone but myself; I could spend my evenings doing whatever my budget and common sense allowed. I was free then, not bound by the very real demands of a home and family.

And yet it's easy to forget that a constant theme throughout my single years was the innate desire for a husband and children, along with the latent fear that they'd never materialize. As much as I enjoyed the freedom to float wherever I wanted, I also knew that I was called to the relationships of marriage and motherhood and that I would find fulfillment there. My life these days is less exotic and exciting than it once was, but on another level, it's far more peaceful; I'm living the life I am called to live, and there's something deeply affirming about that. I can stop worrying about whether I'll ever have a family of my own. I have that life now, and what remains for me is to live it as intentionally and as gratefully as I can.

And this covenant to my kids—that I'll always love you, that I'll always be there for you—is just one more aspect of my life that helps me understand God's promise to me. In the Old Testament, God promises Noah, and promises Abraham, and those promises are fulfilled. There's a satisfaction in knowing that I am bound to my little boys as surely as God is bound to me. I reaffirm this covenant over and over, every time I change a diaper or hug someone after a nightmare or pick up my little preschool scholar after nap and snack. And I like knowing that I am providing two little people with a sense of security, that I am giving them the confident assurance that Mom isn't going anywhere. I hope that, with this security, they can relax and expand into their fullest, strongest, most beautiful selves. I hope that my commitment is helping them grow up to be safe, hopeful, and optimistic about life and the world.

Maybe this is why God made that covenant with us: so that we can exhale and enjoy the world he's created. Instead of worrying about whether we'll be abandoned, we can rest secure in the knowledge that God is in it for the long haul. As a result, we're free to turn our attention to other things; we hope to transform it into creative energy for the good. And I think this process must be as satisfying for God as it is for us.

So I understand now what my colleague meant about marriage and parenthood all those years ago. There's the promise that you say to the guy in a tuxedo on a very memorable day, but that's not the end of it. There is also the promise that you say to the little guy in Velcro sneakers who is hanging onto your leg at the threshold of a classroom, and it's the promise that you repeat day after day in ways that are both spoken and silent. Mommy won't ever forget you or leave you. Mommy always comes back after nap and snack.

And that's not Mommy's burden. It's her privilege.

5
Comfort Zones

Going Past the Place Where I'd Normally Quit

The first time I ever fainted, I was fourteen years old. It happened on a Saturday morning in the back room of a jewelry store. My sister Amy had just turned sixteen, which meant that she was at last old enough, according to my parents' rules, to get her ears pierced. I was there because on this occasion (as on so many) my parents decided that it was simpler for me to get my ears done at the same time than to wait two years and go back. (I've decided that this phenomenon is why younger children often end up spoiled and older children often wind up indignant.)

Anyhow, I did fine during the actual piercing, but as the jewelry-store lady was telling us how to clean the pierce sites with alcohol, I started to feel woozy. Next thing I remember, I was staring at gray carpet about an inch from my face and hearing voices above me saying, "No, don't get up yet." It made for quite a story the next day at school.

That was the first of many fainting episodes. I've lost consciousness three times while watching violent movies, and almost lost it twice in classrooms when we were reading or discussing violent passages of novels (yes, really). I was seconds away from blacking out once while I was having blood drawn, so ever since then I have told lab workers that I need to lie down. I am always humbly apologetic about making them hunt down an available cot, but they assure me that it would be much more trouble to peel me up off the floor.

As far as anyone can tell, this tendency to faint is due to low blood pressure. I think it may also be due to a very vivid imagination, one that can't quite pry itself away from the disturbing thought of a vial of blood teetering there on my arm. With an imagination like this, I'm way too good at internalizing the pain of movie characters who have their hands crushed (*Of Mice and Men*) or their thumbs cut off (*The English Patient*). Something about violence to hands really gets me. I'm a great candidate for psychoanalysis.

So there is a little part of me that always feared becoming a mom. Even though my sister and I were pretty good in this regard—I don't think we ever went to the ER, at least not for a bloody accident—I know that most kids get into scrapes, quite literally. My husband has harrowing childhood stories of hitting his head on the hibachi grill and needing several stitches, and of picking up a bucket that was turned over a wasps' nest and then trying unsuccessfully to escape from the angry critters who, with their puny waspy intellect, decided to attack their own liberator. And I have heard stories of older siblings who have accidentally closed younger siblings' fingers in doors, which is about as much as I can write about that because even *thinking* of that scene makes me feel like getting personal with the floor. So, yes, before having kids, I just hoped that when those accidents happened, I would miraculously make it through without adding an unconscious mom to an already tense situation.

My big test came the summer before Matthew turned three.

It started innocently enough: a Saturday morning trip to the library, with Matthew and nine-month-old Luke sitting side-by-side in the double stroller. As was typical of Matthew at that age, the moment I let him loose in the children's room he was more ready to run than to read. He took off gleefully in the general direction of a wooden bench. I was turning to pick up a board book for Luke, so I did not see the actual moment of contact between boy and bench, but I heard the thud and the ensuing loud scream, and then I turned to see Matthew sprawled on the floor. As I ran toward him, he ran toward me, bawling hysterically, and we met halfway.

There was blood on his lower lip. I held him close to me, and he kept screaming, and I patted his back and tried to get him to pull away so I could look. I finally moved him into my line of vision, and as I did so, I saw that there was a huge bloodstain on my left shoulder, soaking through my shirt. Anyone looking at me would have thought I'd been shot. I looked at my wounded little guy, and I saw that one of Matthew's lower canine teeth had punctured all the way through the skin of his face, making a neat little cut about a quarter-inch below his bottom lip.

I had no idea a tooth could even *do* that. And I could feel the wooziness starting, creeping into my consciousness like a grim fog. Under normal circumstances it was the point at which I'd sit or preferably lie down to stave off a fainting episode, but I could hardly do that with a wounded and wailing little boy in my arms.

Somehow I got Matthew buckled into the other half of the double stroller, and we shot out of the library, bat-out-of-hell style. As we screeched down the ramp, I kept thinking: *I have to keep it together. I have to keep it together. Please God help me do this.* I was terrified that I'd keel over on the wheelchair ramp, my little boys still side by side in their stroller. I had that old feeling of teetering on the precipice of consciousness.

But at the same time, it was like there was another me grabbing my collar from behind and pulling firmly backwards, resisting the plunge. I held on to that feeling with as much strength as I could.

I gripped the stroller handles. I took some of the deepest breaths of my life and said soothing words that I did not actually believe but which seemed, miraculously, to calm Matthew. And by the time I had made it to the car and buckled in the boys, I knew that I had somehow, *some* way, ridden out the wooziness and made it to the other side. That's one advantage of being a frequent fainter: you know when you've gotten through the worst of it. I could tell that I was—thank God—in the clear.

Of course, savoring my personal triumph had to wait. I took the boys to the ER, where we waited for quite a long time in the examining room. The doctor came in to assess the situation, then disappeared again for several minutes, then the nurse came in and gave Matthew a pad of anesthesia to numb his lip, and then we waited fifteen minutes for it to work. I tried hard to keep my scared little boy calm. "Let's play games," I said brightly, looking around the room. It was a cavernous space, with an operating table and all kinds of cabinets and lights and equipment on trolleys, and switches and tubes. Frankly, it was kind of intimidating, even to me. But I made up a little challenge: "I see something red. Can you find the something red that I see?" And Matthew looked around and finally noticed the fire alarm by the door and pointed to it with a big grin underneath his pad of anesthesia, and I said, "Yes! You got it!" And we went several rounds while Luke grew restless in his half of the stroller, and I began to curse the fact that I did not have a bottle for him, because he was, at this point, about an hour overdue for one.

I'll spare you all the details of the actual stitching, mostly because I didn't watch. When a toddler gets facial stitches, he is put into an elaborate and comprehensive restraint system, like a surfboard with a Velcro jacket that binds everything but his head. It was like something out of *One Flew over the Cuckoo's Nest*—pretty painful for a mom to see. But boy, Matthew was a trouper, not even crying as the doctor stitched him up. I stood at his side, looking into his eyes, saying encouraging words and trying hard not to accidentally glance at the needlework going on a few inches away. "Wow, he's amazing," said the doctor. I agreed.

Matthew left the ER with an orange Popsicle melting in his hand and praise ringing in his ears. The Popsicle fell apart in the car when we were a few blocks from home, and his hands were stained orange, and the upholstery got wet, but I couldn't have cared less. If something were going to fall apart that day, better the ice pop than Mom.

Looking back on that day, I have no idea how I got through it without passing out. It flew in the face of my every prior experience with blood and puncture wounds. I'm also not sure how I managed to get through the lengthy ordeal in the ER without losing it. All I can say is that I dug deep like I'd never dug before. But this is what happens when you become a mom: you get to know what you are truly capable of handling. Parenthood is a big old lab, the crucible in which you are tested by fire, over and over, in lots of different ways. It is the place in which you see the stuff that lies there, at your center, when you burn away all the dross.

Sometimes I don't feel so triumphant, there in parent lab. A lot of the time, when I go deep, I'm not so happy with what I find. One day, as Matthew was driving me nuts by whining and not listening and jumping on the bed, and I was getting snappish and mean, I realized that I'm not as patient as I used to be. And then I had to stop and think: *Maybe it's not a question of becoming less patient than before. Maybe I was never really as patient as I thought I was. After all, I've never been tested like this before.* That's a pretty humbling realization. The good news is that it gives me something to work on if I am so inclined (most of the time, I am). And I do believe that self-knowledge, even if it shows you something that disappoints you, is always better than the alternative.

And more and more, because of these experiences, I've started looking at other people in a new light. So many of the folks I admire as role models were put in situations that demanded more of them than they surely felt qualified to give. They had to move out of their comfort zones, and in pretty dramatic ways. My faith community offers a whole string of examples, people whose stories I always accepted readily when I was a kid but who now awe me with the sheer magnitude of what they faced and what they accomplished. I think of Moses, who found himself suddenly in charge of liberating an entire population from an implacably cruel leader. I think of Mary, who agreed to become an unwed mother (scary enough in her time) and also the mother of God. There's Jesus himself, praying the night before his execution, digging deep to get the strength to face what he knows he must face. All these people, when confronted with new and challenging situations, found depths inside themselves that they did not know were there.

A common thread, I think, is that every one of them felt an obligation to someone outside themselves. There was surely a point when they realized that their own formerly accepted boundaries, the places at which they might normally quit, had to be transcended because other people were counting on them. They were part of something larger than themselves and their human weakness, sort of like me with Matthew and the punctured face. And perhaps they—like me—discovered that there's a divine force willing to give us a hand, to help see us through to the end. That in itself is a fascinating question: how much of our triumph comes from our own gutsy leap over the abyss, and how much is due to the wind called God that helps propel us along? There's probably no way to answer that question, and perhaps teasing apart the two factors is not what matters. Maybe what really matters is that in those moments when we take the leap, we choose to have faith that the wind will be there.

It's now three years later, and you can't even see the scar below Matthew's lip. Thanks to OxiClean, the blood washed out of my shirt without leaving a trace. These days, I'm not sure how much Matthew even remembers of the whole episode. Sometimes, when he is doing something risky and likely to put himself in the path of grievous bodily injury, I will say, "Matthew, remember when you hurt your lip and had to go to the doctor? You don't want to do that again, right?" He will suddenly look serious and pensive, which makes me think that he does remember. At any rate, I sure do. I can't pass the library now without thinking of that entire horrible morning, the Velcro surfboard, the blue stitches, and the sheer terror.

I suspect that I have many more tests ahead, of varying degrees; as the mother of two active boys, it pains me to say that we have surely not seen the last of the ER. But next time, I will at least have the memory of a mom who held it together, who fought through the faintness like a lioness, who amused her little boy with an impromptu game while waiting in a strange operating room. And I will have the memory of my little boy, so scared and yet so stoic, who managed to smile at me as he waited with a huge pad of anesthesia strapped to his lip, a little boy who stayed calm while a strange man bent over his face with a big needle and thread. The memory of that brave little face looking out from the elaborate restraints can still make me want to cry.

Because another thing that I always find there at my center, through every challenge and every terror, is a fierce core of mommy love. It is already as strong as it could possibly be, and at the same time, in a fascinating paradox, it just keeps growing stronger.

I think that's the most amazing self-discovery of all.

6

Dying to Self

There's a New Me Coming Out of All This Mess

Parenthood is all about creating and nurturing new life, a process that's wonderful and heady and miraculous. At the risk of sounding terribly grim, though, I have to say that parenthood is also all about death. It's the death of the person you used to be, that carefree spirit who had no one else depending on her. It is often the death of leisure time and disposable income; it's nearly always the death of spontaneity. Before having children, you can decide on a whim to go to dinner and a movie on a Saturday night. After having kids, that outing takes about as much advance planning as a month-long trek in the Alaskan wilderness.

This, I know, is exactly why many people are afraid to have kids. It is why, deep in the innermost chamber of my heart, I was afraid to have kids too. I liked the little life my husband and I had carved out for ourselves. It was not extravagant, and it did not involve wild parties or skydiving, but it did involve a basic freedom. We could, within certain financial limits, do whatever we wanted, whenever we wanted. That narrow little Mediterranean restaurant on Fillmore that we loved? We could breeze in unencumbered, without having to wedge a stroller or high chair between the tables. We could spend

an evening with good friends without having to break the conversation to run after a toddler who was about to bite into an electrical
cord. Some of our friends who had gotten a few years' head start on
us in the family department demonstrated the joy of becoming parents, but also the challenges. Our times with them were different:
more frenzied and less leisurely. "Remember when we used to just
sit around the living room and talk?" I asked one of my friends at
a party, and she laughed hollowly as her young son raced by, seated
on an absurdly small toy fire truck. It was hard to imagine giving up
all that.

And when you have kids, you know that you *will* give it up. It's
more than a fair trade; I'd become a mom all over again, in a heartbeat. At the same time, I don't do myself any favors if I try to sug-
arcoat the fact that parenthood means making some pretty major
sacrifices that I don't always feel like making. When my son wakes
me up at four in the morning because he has an earache, as much as
I feel awful for my miserable little boy, I also feel awful that I have to
get up again in two hours' time and stand in front of a classroom of
students and be coherent. I tend to pine enviously for the way I used
to be able to sleep all night—*all* night!—without interruption. For
me, then, it helps to acknowledge silently that this is a little death
and that, yes, the whole experience does stink. But—and this is the
crucial step—I then remind myself that there is a larger meaning to
it, a meaning that redeems it and makes it less deathlike.

And that's the part that counts.

There's a phrase I've come across often in Catholic thought and doc-
trine: *dying to self.* I once hated this term. It used to make me think
of old-school, guilt-based Catholicism, which I have spent much
of my early adult life trying to transcend. When religious writings

admonished me to "die to self," I took it to mean that, as an individual, I did not matter, that I had to give up my very personality and become a religious robot. It never made sense to me that God would make us all so wonderfully unique and then ask us to trim away all the lovely individual quirks, turning us into the human equivalent of Soviet-style bloc housing.

But now that I'm a mom, I see the phrase entirely through the lens of sacrifice. When you are a parent, you *do* die to yourself, over and over and over. You die to your desire to watch a TV show uninterrupted. You die to the long-awaited dinner with girlfriends that suddenly has to be given over to an impromptu visit to the pediatric after-hours clinic. You die to the fact that you can't go shopping for bras because that would involve trying them on, and you happen to have two small boys with you. Every day you get to experience at least one little death. Most days, you experience a lot of them.

And as depressing as all this sounds, here's the good part: acknowledging that it is a death actually helps me. Because most things that are meaningful come with some sort of a price. And the whole point behind dying to self is that the death is not an endpoint. It always helps facilitate a higher purpose, some positive outcome, some resurrection that you may not be able to see right away. There are times when I'm so resentful of losing all my old free-independent-me time that I never quite make it to that realization. But if I can get myself out of the pity party and look at the long view, I know that what I have given up in this whole parenting gig is pretty minor compared with what I am gaining.

When you are a mom or a dad, happiness is a tricky thing to quantify. Periodically I'll see a headline about how some new scientific study has shown that parents are happier than nonparents, or vice versa. I'm not a research scientist, but I always struggle to understand how anyone can actually measure parental happiness. This is not pond water we're talking about; you can't dip a vial into a random stretch of parenting, pull it up, and assume you've got a representative sample of the whole. Every day—and every week, every month, every year—is going to be different from the one that came before and from the one that will come after. Even if you happen to be smack in the middle of the most challenging period of your life as a mom, something lovely can be growing below the surface, being nudged along little by little, and you can sense that it's there, and you know that it will burst into flower later, and the thought of that gives you a certain peace. And even during those times of diaper explosions and high fevers and bratty attitudes, when parenting is as far from fun as you can possibly get, most parents still recognize that this calling to which they have pledged their lives is fundamentally a meaningful and good thing. "There is a difference between happiness and satisfaction," said my dad once. "Parenting does not always make you happy, but it does give you satisfaction." I'm a rookie at this game, compared with my dad, who is thirty-six years ahead of me. But I'm beginning to see how right he is.

And the great thing about parenting is that every now and then, you get a random burst of joy that leaves you breathless. There's the smile that I get from Luke, a toothy coy grin, his head cocked to one side, his coffee-colored eyes roguish and sweet; it pierces my heart like an arrow and more than makes up for having to scrub away the nearly indelible food stains on the baseboards by his high chair. You have to stack up a lot of dirty clothes to equal the electric joy I get at the end of a preschool day when Matthew runs toward me, laughing and calling, "Mommy!" You can't really describe those moments, and you can't quantify them either. All you can say is that they make every little death worthwhile.

If there were a way to parent without the sacrifice, I'd be all for it. But the universe doesn't work that way. I've died to many aspects of

my former self, and I continue to do so, like every time I am awak-
ened out of a delicious weekend morning slumber by Luke yelling
"Mommy? Daddy? I want to get up!" from the next room. I try to
block it out, hoping to buy myself another few moments of sleep,
but it never works. I haul myself out of bed, fumble for my slippers,
and shuffle into his room.

But there is a new me that is coming out of all of this death. It's
the me who can be rendered speechless with joy by the touch of a
small hand, still warm from the blankets, that instinctively reaches
for mine.

7
Mindfulness
This, Too, Shall Pass

For an English-teacher nerd like me, going to the Oregon Shakespeare Festival in Ashland, Oregon, is pretty much like entering paradise. I went for the first time as a teenager, when my great-aunt Carol took me with her one summer. Then I was lucky enough to go both junior and senior years with my high school Shakespeare club. It was a thrill to stay in a motel, to wander around the small town with my friends and join up with the teacher chaperones for meals, to see plays by Shakespeare and Ibsen and modern playwrights. And, of course, there were so many cute actors to moon over from afar. They'd never have gone for Catholic-school jailbait like us, but still, it was fun to dream.

During my senior year, one of the plays we saw was *Our Town* by Thornton Wilder. It's an undisputed classic, a look at small-town America in the early 1900s as narrated by an endearing, wise character called the Stage Manager. The first two acts are sweet; we see the budding courtship of teenage Emily and her neighbor George, and then their wedding day.

And then, in the third act, there is a shift. Emily has died as a young woman, and she's given the chance to come back, just for a day, to the town and family she used to know. She chooses to relive the morning of her twelfth birthday. And the experience of it is too much for her to bear. Nothing else has changed but herself. She relives every moment of that day with the perspective of someone who knows, from personal experience, that life is finite.

There's a famous moment when she asks, through her tears, "Do any human beings ever realize life while they live it . . . every, every minute?" And the Stage Manager, with his gentle wisdom, answers, "No. The saints and poets, maybe—they do some."

When the curtain went up on the play that winter's day in Ashland, I applauded politely. It was a good play and a solid production; the story, I felt, was hardly earth-shattering. But I looked over at Mr. Christensen, my English teacher, and I noticed that he had tears in his eyes.

Later, during our debriefing back at the hotel, most of us seniors were of the same mind: a nice play and an enjoyable one, but not dramatic. Not on the scale of, say, Shakespeare's tragedies. Mr. Christensen listened to us and shook his head. "Maybe you can't really appreciate *Our Town* until you are older, until you have kids of your own," he said.

I'm beginning to think he was right.

When you are the mother of small children, the days at home just crawl by. I've learned that one advantage to being a working mom is that you do get to leave the house daily and interact with people who can construct complex sentences, people who don't require you to hover in the doorway as they use the toilet. But because my work life follows the school year, there are many summer days when I'm home with the boys from morning till night. I'm not complaining about those precious weeks off. Still, those days at home move much more slowly than my times in the classroom. I often find myself thinking hard for ways to absorb the morning hours: *Let's go for a walk! Let's go to the post office! We'll take a trip to Trader Joe's, even if we don't really need anything!* And so I make the slow march toward nap time, which, naturally, goes by at twice the speed of the rest of the day. And then the boys wake up, and I get juice, settle toy disputes, and make dinner while longing, more or less, for the boys' bedtime and some precious quiet time to myself.

And that's on a good day. I won't even get into the bad days, when Matthew is set on automatic whine and Luke seems to want no other toy in the house but the one in his older brother's hands, the days when someone has a pee pee accident or vomits directly into the train bin. On those days, I just hang on tight and pray for deliverance.

"Remember what Grandma always used to say," my aunt told me when she happened to call after just such a day.

"Remind me."

"She always used to say 'This, too, shall pass,'" my aunt said. "If I was having a bad day with the kids, she'd say 'Nothing ever lasts forever. Look in the Bible. The Bible always says "And it came to pass." It never says "And it came to stay."'"

"Grandma was a smart lady," I said.

This, too, shall pass. I remind myself of that as I count the crawling minutes until bedtime. This evening with its endless monotony, broken only by sibling squabbles, shall pass. Or sometimes, I pull the lens back and go even broader: This year will pass. Someday the boys will be older, more mature, able to entertain themselves. Someday I'll be able to take them to Trader Joe's and Luke won't grab vitamin bottles off the shelves as I wheel him past in the stroller. I see other mothers in the store with their boys, older boys of eight, nine, or ten, and I think: *Just imagine when Matthew and Luke are that age. Just imagine when I can tell them I need some time to myself and I can close the bedroom door and write or pray or read, confident that I won't come back out to find that they've played Picasso on the dining-room wall. Just imagine when I can send them out to the back-yard to play without having to be there myself, standing watch, making sure they don't find and sample the one rogue mushroom springing out of the lawn.*

This, too, shall pass. It's a comforting thought. But at the same time, it's an agonizing thought. Because when Matthew is ten, will he still have the endearing cowlick that sticks straight out of the back of his head like a cock's comb? When Luke is eight, will he still have that deep, guttural laugh that makes me break into a smile every time? I know that he will no longer have that baby-soft skin, a chunky little stretch of bare leg visible between his socks on one end and the edge of his shorts on the other. He will probably be long and lean and gangly, that cuddly frame just a memory. And when Matthew is ten, will he still want me to read him bedtime stories, snuggled up against me on the sofa? I read to him every night, and because I'm a book nerd and a closet actress, it can be remarkably fun. Even so, there are many evenings when I'm in a rush, turning to the next page before I've even finished reading the one I'm on. Sometimes he'll choose a story that is long and involved, and I groan inside, just wishing that I could get him quickly to bed so that my own life—my own independent me-life—can start again. I can't wait for those precious two or three hours to myself, with no small boy making demands on my time.

But really, what am I wanting to rush? I can't have the sweet cowlick and chunky legs without the three-year-old attitude and the tantrums. It would be great to tease them apart and isolate the good, but that's just a fantasy. I cannot accelerate the bad while slowing down the good.

And that good . . . well, it speeds by. Sometimes I don't realize how quickly time is passing until someone—a family member from out of state, an old friend—sees the boys after a long absence and comments on how grown-up Matthew is, with his ability to carry on a conversation, or how much Luke is looking like a little boy, not like a baby anymore. Those comments always make me stop, look at my own kids anew, and notice what has slipped by, unrecognized, in the string of days as they passed. They are not the same little boys they were just a few months ago. I have to face this even when I'm folding laundry. I adored folding all those soft little sleepers that both boys wore as babies, the green and yellow and blue jammies printed with dogs and gentle giraffes. But the sleepers are gone now, given away to other pregnant friends. I've saved a few little pieces that I can't bear to part with, but we're on to bigger clothes now, smaller versions of what my husband wears. The boys will never wear those giraffe sleepers again.

This, too, shall pass. Often that mantra is a comfort, just as my grandma intended it to be. But more and more, it's also a wake-up call. It's a reminder that the days that seem endless run into months that pass in a shot. And once they go, I will never get them back.

That's something my grandma understood. Maybe, as she gave that advice to my frazzled aunt, she was thinking of it from both angles. My grandma died when I was sixteen, after a prolonged battle with breast cancer, and she was not one who took happiness for granted. This attitude was not just a result of her illness; I suspect that she had cultivated it early in her life. After a painful childhood, she married at nineteen and had a long, happy marriage with my grandfather, with whom she was extremely well matched. I often wonder if the difficult circumstances of her early life made her more grateful than most for the small pleasures she encountered later. More than most people I know, she took joy in little things. When we went to their house for dinner, she'd take my mom out to the yard to show her the latest blooms on the gardenia by the back door. She'd show me a pretty card that an old friend had sent her: "Look at that! Isn't that a beautiful postcard?" Many people would just drop it in the trash, but not Grandma. After we had spent an evening with them, she'd send me a note on flowered notepaper, full of her signature dashes, as if she were thinking with her pen. "Grandpa and I loved seeing you yesterday—you played the piano so beautifully—and what fun to see your new Heidi doll!" It was Grandma capturing the experience by putting it into writing, a way that she kept those memories alive for herself and, certainly, for me.

I am not a poet, exactly, and I'm most emphatically not a saint. But it's fair to say that I'm finally learning what I could not have known my senior year of high school, sitting in a darkened Ashland theater. Time passes. Life is finite. There is no kindly Stage Manager to give me another chance to live the day of my choice.

And if I did get that chance, what would I choose? Much as I loved my wedding day, I wouldn't choose that one; nor would I choose the birth of either son, heady and thrilling as those events were. Instead, I would choose a day much like today: chaotic, exhausting, messy, and not especially noteworthy, a day when I microwaved chicken dinos, mopped up spilled milk, and stepped over scattered building blocks. And when Matthew chose a book to read before bed, I'd hope it was a long one. I would linger on every page, encouraging him to ask questions about the illustrations. When Luke ran up to me while I composed an email, I would not absently touch his head and type on. I'd get up from the table, pick him up, and swing him around in circles. He'd guffaw with joy, and I'd laugh too, spinning in the air until my arms ached with his weight and I could not possibly hold him anymore.

8

Those Who Came Before

Planting the Seeds

When my husband and I moved into our house about eight years ago, I knew instinctively that something was missing. It had lovely mature Japanese maples out back, an extra room we could use as an office, and a charming 1940s-era phone nook in the hallway, which I happily commandeered for use as a Mary shrine.

But it didn't have a garden. The yard was thick with shrubs, and the trees were tall and graceful, but other than a tough dark pink camellia in the back corner, there were no flowers. And that felt wrong.

I'm sure that not every homeowner would have been so affronted by the lack of blooms, but then, not every homeowner was raised by my mother. When I was a kid, our backyard was always vivid with color: begonias or impatiens in the shade, marigolds around the birdbath in the center of the lawn, lobelia and geraniums and azaleas in pots on the patio. Over the years, I spent more than a few hours going with Mom on expeditions to the nursery, where we'd wander the aisles, pausing periodically to add a plastic six-pack of annuals to the cart. Mom's love of flowers was not limited just to the ones in her own yard; anytime we were out on walks, she'd exclaim over the plants we passed, calling them by name, sometimes bending in for a close encounter. This caused more than a little embarrassment for my sister and me during our teenage years. Trips to the supermarket often involved my mom sniffing rapturously at the flowers growing in the parking lot median strips, while Amy and I ducked our heads and pretended not to know her.

If you ask my mom how she came by this love of flowers, she'll give the credit entirely to her mom, my Grandma Wolf. Grandma's yard has always been a little Eden of hydrangeas, fuchsias, the occasional hollyhock reaching for the sky, and honeysuckle spilling over the fence. Though Grandma is now in her nineties, she still lives at home, and for her, a good day is a day spent digging in the soil. She is thrilled that I've taken to gardening, and her birthday and Christmas gifts often have an outdoors theme: new garden gloves; seed packets of nasturtiums or forget-me-nots; a small stone duck with a curled ribbon around its neck. Her notes, written by hand, often include a report on her garden: "Lots of weeding lately. The front yard is blooming again, it looks so pretty." In my notes to her, I always include a report on the status of my own flower beds: the marigolds I planted, the roses just starting to bloom. Next to news about me and the boys, I know that these are the kinds of updates my grandma loves most.

The older I get, the more I realize that much of what I love—much of what I am—is due to the people who came before me. The way that Mom and Grandma chose to spend their time and their treasure—turning the soil, weeding, buying flats of annuals and the inevitable box of snail bait—has shown me that there is value in making one little patch of the planet more lovely to look at. From them, I've learned the intoxicating scent of dark brown soil, the pleasure of patting it down around a tiny plant and feeling it give under my gloves, elastic and loose and full of promise. Without

Mom and Grandma's instinctive habit of commenting delightedly on the flowers they pass, I would not know how to tell a begonia from a primrose. Without their enthusiasm, my life would lack the delicious flights of imagination evoked by the mere names of certain flowers, like the purplish Lilies of the Nile in my parents' backyard. It's fair to say that without Mom and Grandma, I probably would not be who I am today: a woman whose fingers itch to turn the soil and paint the yard with color.

Just recently, on a mild Saturday morning, I invited the boys to help me plant pansies in the front yard. I gave each boy a trowel, and they dug happily in the dirt, creating small holes for the tiny flowers (and, eventually, for their Matchbox cars). They enjoyed it immensely; Luke loves anything to do with dirt, and Matthew is a great enthusiast when it comes to watering. I was far less efficient with the boys there than I would have been working alone; more than once, I had to stop the boys from dumping dirt directly on the pansies. But it was worth the extra effort to have them there, sharing the sunny spring morning.

A few days later, in a card to my grandma, I told her about Matthew and Luke and their trowels and their cars and their enthusiasm. I knew it would make her happy to know that the seeds she planted in my mom and in me are blooming all over again in two busy little boys.

Throughout my life, I've been lucky to have close relationships with my grandparents. Though my Grandpa Wolf died of a heart attack when I was only a few months old, the other three were a huge part of my childhood. Grandma Wolf lived in Santa Barbara, a six-hour drive away; with her, we had the fun of frequent visits on the train and by car and the excitement of having her come to stay with us as well. (It was always fun to walk to the nearby doughnut store and watch Mom and Grandma argue about who would pay. Grandma invariably won.) Grandma and Grandpa Kubitz lived about a forty-five minute drive away, close enough for them to attend birthday parties and dance recitals and various sacraments. Their presence always made these events feel even more like celebrations.

And over the past few years, it's been a treat to see my parents, and Scott's parents, in the role of grandparents to my young sons. All four of them love building memories with Matthew and Luke. I find it fascinating to see which memories they are choosing to create.

Take my father and trains. As a kid, my dad dreamed of having a Lionel toy train, something that was beyond his family's means. It was only after retirement that he began collecting trains, and the timing of this coincided nicely with the birth of his first grandson, whom Dad was determined to mold into a fellow enthusiast. He pursued this goal with relentless energy; when Matthew was only a few weeks old, Dad came over for dinner one evening with a Lionel toy train DVD in hand for the evening's entertainment. When the engines went up for Matthew's first Christmas, Dad would take baby Matthew on his lap, and they would sit there, silently and content-edly, watching the little train go round and round the tree. It was Dad and Mom who gave Matthew his first little wooden Thomas the Tank Engine figurines, when he was still at least a year away from actually being able to play with them. With full-court-press indoctrination like this, Matthew's future as a locomotive enthusiast was pretty much guaranteed, and he has more than delivered. (For years, his favorite prayer at night has been to ask Jesus to watch over Grandpa's trains.) And now that he and Luke are old enough to run the train themselves, the Christmas season finds the boys sitting on their haunches by the track, my dad hovering nearby, taking turns with the remote and making the little engine chug-chug-chug along.

All three are totally rapt. All three are loving it. And all three are building a store of memories.

Scott's parents, who live in upstate New York, have exposed the boys to special places. When we make our annual summertime visit, our little California boys (and their California mom) have the chance to experience the landscape that is so much a part of their grandparents' life. On the shores of Otsego Lake, a beautiful heaven of forests and water and rock, Grandma Joan will take the boys outside for slow, unhurried walks. They look at wildflowers and sometimes pick them, bringing them into the house and placing them in little cups of water on the kitchen windowsill. Sometimes we pack up the boys and a huge bag full of sand toys and head over to the stretch of beach at the far end of the lake, where they spend a morning playing in a setting that is indescribably beautiful. On our last visit, we all went out on a rented boat, the boys wearing stiff orange life vests. Grandpa Bob steered the boat and let the boys sit on his lap, hands on the wheel, as the wind whipped their short hair and they surveyed the water with pride, two tiny little captains. This part of the world has been home to my father-in-law for most of his life; his roots here are deep. And for a Californian who is new to the lake culture of the East, it's a treat for me to learn the joy of a day spent on a boat on a beautiful body of water. I can see how much this landscape and these experiences mean to my father-in-law, who once owned a boat of his own and who has lifelong memories of summer days spent on or near the water.

Now my sons have those memories, too. They are going to carry with them the memory of how exciting it is to see the rocky banks scroll past them, banks that are full of history and legend. They are going to know how it feels to see the sun bounce off the water, to hear the cries of the gulls, to exclaim at the beauty of the lake only to have the wind take the words right out of your mouth, passing them to the person behind you.

This is what they do, the generations who come before us: they expose us to the things they love. We see and experience and learn. Some of it sticks, and some of it doesn't. But there is a powerful witness in valuing something enough to want to pass it along to the next generation. That desire to share, to keep something alive for our kids and grandkids, shows those of us on the receiving end that perhaps there is something there that is worth our respect and worthy of our love. In my life as a parent, I have seen how this is true of trains and gardening and summer days on the lake. I have also seen how it's true of faith.

Both of our boys were baptized very early, when they were barely a month old. There were a few reasons for this. My husband works in ministry, and I write about spirituality; church geeks that we are, we really couldn't wait to pass the faith along to our boys. By fast-tracking the baptisms, we were also able to make sure that Scott's parents, visiting from the East, could be there for the big day.

There are clear challenges to scheduling a baptism when your child is a month old. When you are hardly sleeping more than a few hours in a row, when your life has been systematically overhauled by a very small and demanding new family member, getting your head around planning a sacrament and a reception is quite the feat. (So, too, is finding a dressy outfit that can fit over your still huge postpartum middle).

And when Matthew was born, we had the extra challenge of what to do about a christening gown. As far as I knew, there were no family heirlooms on either side, but I checked with both grandmas just to be sure. And much to my surprise, Mom produced a short linen gown with a tiny round collar. It had short puffed sleeves and miniscule buttons. The cloth was once white but had turned ivory over many years spent in the cedar chest. It's the baptism gown that my father wore when he was baptized in Chicago in 1940, and I did not know it existed until Mom gave it to me.

"Do you think this gown will work for the baptism?" Mom asked.

"Yes," I told her. "It's perfect."

I was thrilled that Matthew would get to wear a garment with a family history, and not just because it meant I didn't have to traipse around the stores trying to find one. Baptism, really, is all about relationships. It's about consciously choosing to connect your child's life to the lives of others. If you are baptizing your child in the faith of your parents and grandparents, you are continuing a tradition that has gone on for generations, unrolling through time like a beautiful bolt of cloth. If you are baptizing your child in a faith that you chose for yourself, you are making the choice to connect with other lives, with a community, in a very profound and familial way. Either way, you are making an implicit statement that you have something in your life that you care about enough to pass along to your child, a faith that you hope will function as a point of origin, a touchstone in a world that constantly changes.

It's taken me a while to be able to say this, but I'm profoundly grateful that my parents baptized me. This was not always the case. I didn't want much to do with Catholicism once I hit college, a time when I was fairly critical of organized religion in general. But when I came back to the practice of my faith during my midtwenties, I was tremendously glad that I had something to come back to. The faith my parents had chosen for me was the place where I felt at home. In my Catholic life was a store of good memories that had never gone away: parish events, May crownings, Easter Masses, lovely moments in prayer, an awareness of the innate dignity of human life, a belief that there were things in this world larger than I was but which could, somehow, still make themselves small enough for me to hold.

I wanted Matthew to have that storehouse of memories too, memories to sustain him throughout all the phases of his spiritual journey.

And I loved knowing that the first step of that journey would be taken in the same gown that my father wore when he took his.

So we carefully pressed the little gown, and Matthew wore it for his big day. Two years later, in the same church, Luke wore it, too. Once again, all four grandparents were in attendance. Once again, there was the joy I felt at knowing that I was giving my little boy a history, a family of faith, an identity that he would share with so many people who came before.

And both times, as I held my little boys, I thought of Dad's mom, my Grandma Kubitz. Unlike me, she had never gone through a period where she stopped practicing her faith. Growing up with an alcoholic mother and a father who was unable to cope with his wife's addiction, she had held on to Catholicism as a constant, something dependable, a source of comfort. For a time, her parents sent her to live in a convent school run by nuns, and she thrived there. When I was a teenager, we moved her to tears one day by surprising her with a statue of Mary for her garden. It reminded her of the statue at the convent school, one she had loved as a child. She died when I was sixteen, and even now, I think of her often and miss her terribly.

But I felt her presence quite near on the days that Matthew and Luke were baptized. As I held my little boys and watched them being welcomed into the faith, I thought about how Grandma would have held Dad, long before he was my father, long before he was a grandfather. She would have dressed him in the same little thin gown and seen the water being poured over his head and smelled the oil as it anointed him. Maybe she thought about the faith that meant so much to her, the comfort it gave to a life that had been marked by so much pain. By baptizing her little boy, she was planting the seed of that faith, passing along the thing that had brought her joy. And that wish, that prayer, felt very close to my heart.

I'm not naive enough to assume that the boys' faith life will end up at exactly the same place where it began. If my own experience has taught me anything, it's that our spiritual journeys can include lots of bends and turns, some of them unexpected. But whatever the future holds, I want my sons to know that once upon a time, they wore a small gown that connected them with those who came before, and with the hopes and love of people they never got the chance to meet. I want them to know there is a gift in being part of a community that involves past, present, and future. And I want them to know that if I had to take all the hopes that I had at their baptisms and distill them into one wish, it would be this:

I hope that the seeds of this faith bloom as colorfully in their lives as they have in mine.

9
The Good and the Bad

You Can't Have One Without the Other

Because we live in California, less than an hour's drive from the ocean, it would be easy to assume that my family spends lots of time at the beach. Actually, given our track record, we might as well be living in Kansas. Due to a combination of inertia, general busyness, and the daunting specter of coastal traffic, my boys were five and three before they had their first encounter with the Pacific Ocean.

The initiation took place on a November afternoon, a day that was slightly chilly and overcast. The sun occasionally broke through a rift in the clouds, beaming down linear rays that made the sky look like a picture on an old holy card. Scott parked the car, and we met up with Matthew's preschool buddy and his parents, who had invited us to go tide pooling. The boys were elated to be seeing each other in a new context, and jumped up and down with glee. We climbed down the wooden steps built into the side of the hill and crossed the beach, heading for the russet-colored kelpy stretch of tide pools. The cool air was bracing and smelled phenomenally good; the afternoon light was mesmerizing; the boys were thrilled; it was shaping up to be one of those memories that I'd want to treasure, to polish and house forever in the curio cabinet of my mind.

And then we got out to the tide pools themselves, and it all fell apart. Matthew and his friend scampered dexterously over the rocky ribs of the pools, peering into the water, pointing to different creatures and listening raptly to the other dad, a veteran tide pooler, as he drew their attention to the marine life inside. But Luke—three-year-old Luke, our little guy with the exuberance of a puppy and the grace of Godzilla—wanted to run with the big kids. He did not want to hold our hands as we led him over the slick, rocky surfaces. Scott and I did not want to let him run roughshod over the fragile ecosystems in which we were, after all, Brobdingnagian visitors. And when the irresistible force of a three-year-old's desires meets the old immovable object of his parents' environmental consciousness, something has to give. That something was my vision of a tranquil, magical time at the beach.

For most of the next hour, Luke was a very unhappy tide pooler. Scott and I took turns carrying him in our arms or trying to put him down on his feet, gripping his hand tightly while he fought wildly to be free. He cried and kicked. He screamed, "I don't want it!" His nose ran copiously, and I realized that I had no Kleenex in the pocket of the old green coat I was wearing. All I could find was a balled pair of unwashed nylon trouser socks, and having these offensive objects rubbed under his nose did little to help Luke's mood. (Who can blame him?) Matthew and his buddy scampered along, being alternately silly and fascinated, thrilled with the landscape and each other. Luke screamed the primal cry of the universe, a cry that was probably loud enough to wake the marine creatures in their watery beds.

"I'm so sorry," said the other mom at one point, looking at me with deep sympathy. "I'm sorry this is such a disaster."

"It's not a disaster, truly," I said. "I'm having a good time." And you know what? I actually was.

Yes, it would have been preferable if Luke were compliant and quiet. But even with his screams playing on a constant loop, I could still notice the beauty of the sky. I could be still and pause and register the fascinating creatures in the pools: the chartreuse sea anemones, looking like flowers from a Dr. Seuss story ("sea enemies," Matthew called them); the small black shell that suddenly moved sideways, propelled by the tiny crab inside; the occasional brown starfish with raised white dots patterning its surface, like the icing piped on a gingerbread cookie. Even with Luke's wails, I could still hear the dramatic crash of the waves as they broke up against the rocks, sending plumes of spray into the air. It was a mix of the bad and the good, all at once, in the same setting and the same afternoon. I could endure the bad while still acknowledging and enjoying the good. And in that way, it was a perfect snapshot of parenthood and of life in general—and, really, of everything in this world that matters.

Long ago I used to be far more dualistic in my thinking than I am now. When I was a kid, there was good, and there was bad. It was a fairy tale world: Snow White was all kindness, and the queen was all evil. If there was someone I admired—a historical figure, a celebrity—I expected her to be irreproachable through and through; even a minor scandal was enough to topple her from the pedestal. I was too young to accept that no one is perfect, that we all have our shadow sides, and that everyone aside from God is going to be disappointing at one time or another.

Somewhere along the way I grew out of this, and my world became one in which I recognized the many shades between black and white. I recognized that we all are paradoxes, each of us containing multitudes, as Walt Whitman once wrote. I also discovered that this is true not just of people but of pretty much everything in the universe. Parenthood is stark proof that the fulfilling and the frustrating dwell very close to each other, often inhabiting the same space. At times, being a mom has made my soul soar; at other times, it has brought me to my knees. It has made me think that I am blessed and privileged to do the glorious job of raising another person, and it has made me feel that some evil fairy has cursed me to a life in which I cannot spend one minute answering an email without having to break up a heated dispute over a toy train. And sometimes these feelings follow so closely on the heels of each other that I feel slightly disoriented or crazy, as if I'm a woman who doesn't even know her own mind anymore.

I distinctly remember one evening when Matthew was a toddler and he spontaneously came up to me and grabbed me in a hug and said, "Mommy, I love you." I squeezed his little body and drank in the smell of his hair and felt love wash over me. Not five minutes later, he was sitting in the timeout corner for kicking me.

Disorienting? Yes. But that's how it is. And if anything, this acceptance that life will hold both the good and the bad, sometimes all at once, is a worldview that we must grow into if we want to have more than a kindergartner's-eye view of the universe. Nothing out there, aside from God, is perfect all the time.

My teaching job is one example. There are days when I am totally on, when I feel like some dynamic hybrid of Robin Williams and Ms. Jean Brodie. Then there are days when leading a discussion feels like extracting teeth—my own teeth, no less, and without anesthesia. But I've taught long enough to realize that you don't let those disaster days define you. You learn from them, you absorb them into the big picture, and you recognize that you still believe that what you do has meaning.

For an example closer to home, there's my relationship with Scott. Years ago, I heard a priest give a presentation in which he talked about how marriage isn't all roses and romance. "That's why you take a vow: because marriage isn't always easy," he said. "If it *were* always easy, you wouldn't need a vow." There's so much truth in that. I happen to be married to the very best man for me, a man who complements me in ways I didn't know I needed complementing. He is brilliant and kind and handsome and funny and roasts absolutely killer coffee. But he would happily go until Judgment Day without making the bed, and he snores (to be fair, he tells me that I do, too), and his logical, engineering-type brain sees the world in ways that are far different from my English-Romantic-poetry brain. There are times when I am utterly grateful for his rational way of moving through life. Then again, there are times when I want him to wax poetic about the new haircut I got, and he doesn't even notice it. And there are days when I want him to intuit from our phone conversation that I have been having a rough day and it would be a great time to show up with a bouquet of flowers, and not being a mind reader, he comes home empty-handed. Does this make me wonder if I married the wrong person? No, because I've learned that even the person you love madly, the person to whom you've committed your life and to whom you'd happily commit it all over again, is not going to hit a home run every time. And accepting that is the first step toward maturity.

Even the practice of my faith has shown itself to be a study in paradox. There are the moments of intense communion with the divine, and then there are long dry spells in which prayer seems more like going through the motions. There are people in this church whose words and actions give me an intoxicating sense of the largeness of God, and there are those whose words and actions seem determined to stuff God into a matchbox. There are the challenging, subversive words of Christ, and then there are the inane platitudes that are often spouted in his name. It's the good and the bad, all mixed together in my experience of faith. Of course, there's a difference between what is bad in the sense of disappointing and what is actually evil. The sex-abuse scandals made it clear that some leaders in the church were willing to tolerate unconscionable acts, and the consequences of that are beyond heartbreaking. But when it comes to my own daily practice of the faith, I've discovered that the disappointment of a dull homily is not enough to make me throw in the towel, nor is an attempt at prayer that feels so arid that I end up bagging it all and watching a rerun of *Frasier*. My faith does, as a whole, bring me joy, even if it does not always make me joyful. Things in this life ebb and flow. Nothing hits the mark every time.

And when I think about this in relation to parenting, I can see how other spiritual beliefs are there to help. There's the value of sacrifice, which helps you grit your teeth and slog on through the bad times. There's the parenting covenant, which is what keeps you there at the shore with your screaming child instead of grabbing the car keys, vaulting into the driver's seat, and blazing down Highway 1, alone and free, with the wind in your hair. And perhaps there is something to be said for contrast—the disappointments that make the gratifying moments that much sweeter by comparison.

And the truth is that even a screaming child can't scream forever. As the afternoon at the tide pools wore on, Luke's wails gradually tapered off. When we left the pools and headed back over the sand, we could finally let go of his hand, and he scampered off to join the two big boys, with no little creatures underfoot to crush. It was evening, and the sun was setting gradually, a disk sinking below the horizon, washing the sky in baby blue and coral pink. The four parents stood talking, watching our boys tumble in the sand. Calm reigned.

It had been a day of extremes: the stormy sobs of Luke contrasted with the gentle peace of the tide pools. But now there were the giggles and squeals of three little boys chasing one another and rolling along the beach, dusted with sand like sugar doughnuts. And in the background was the rhythmic sound of the sea as the waves came in and went out, came in and went out, a sound that echoes a fundamental truth of the universe. You take it all when you're a parent, the crest and the crash, because you can't have one without the other.

10

Mystery

Knowing What I Don't Know

One Sunday Mass, not so long ago, the priest was giving a homily about the importance of listening to the divine. "What we need to do is to be open, to open our hearts to God," he said.

At this, Matthew, who was pushing his Matchbox cars around the seats, suddenly scooted over to me with the look of one who has something urgent to say. "We can't open our hearts," he said, "because we have bones."

I pulled him closer. "What?"

"We can't open our hearts," he said patiently, "because we are mammals. We have bones and things."

"No, honey," I said, trying not to smile. "That's not what the priest means." I cast about for a way to explain it. "Opening your heart to God means listening to God, loving him, and wanting to hear what he has to say. It doesn't mean actually opening up your heart."

Matthew, pondering this, went back to his cars. I settled back into my seat for the rest of the homily, but I found myself distracted by a few thoughts.

Thought One: Wow, that preschool tuition is totally worth it.

Thought Two: Matthew actually listens during Mass. (Who knew?)

Thought Three: This is the first time I have ever explained the concept of figurative language to my son.

As a high school English teacher, I have a lot of direct experience with discussing figurative language. It's always fun to teach; high school students are already aware of the difference between literal and figurative meaning, even if they haven't heard those terms, and it's easy for them to recognize how they use it in their own lives. "When you tell your friends you spent a thousand hours on your math homework last night, did you really *mean* that?" I'll ask. (Yes, some student always says plaintively.) Shakespeare's plays are a fantastic way to explore this kind of language. When we read *Romeo and Juliet*, I'll often have my students choose a metaphor, simile, or personification, then illustrate its literal meaning. The next day, students bring earnest drawings of shining suns with copious eyelashes and long hair ("It is the east, and Juliet is the sun."). And the students are great at identifying the reasons for using such language. Well, it means that she's bright; she's beautiful; she is the center of Romeo's universe; she makes everything seem light. High school students get it.

But four year olds? Not so much.

I can remember a time when I, too, was young enough to take every expression at face value. When I was in kindergarten or thereabouts, my mom was talking to a friend about an acquaintance who had had a heart attack. I immediately envisioned that woman standing in a field as unseen archers shot arrows into her chest.

It's very good to be beyond such basic misunderstandings. And I smile at Matthew's sweet endearing misinterpretations, signs of his innocence and youth. I smile as one who knows all the answers, which is pretty much how he sees me.

But that incident at Mass got me thinking. It is nice to feel like Mom Who Knows All, but that is a fallacy. In the realm of the spiritual, there is a part of me that is still very much on Matthew's level. When it comes to the whys and wherefores of life—especially the reasons bad things happen—I'm no smarter than a four-year-old.

On the journey into motherhood, my husband and I met death. My first pregnancy was an ectopic pregnancy, in which the fetus implants itself in the fallopian tube and not in the uterus. It was an excruciating experience, physically and emotionally. The grief at our loss was sharp and unrelenting.

After several months of physical healing and a great deal of nervousness, we tried to conceive again. We were lucky enough to become pregnant within a few months. I was on tenterhooks until the first ultrasound at six weeks, when the screen showed a little embryo, successfully seated in my uterus. I was radiantly happy. Scott and I called the baby Yokel, a name inspired by my ob/gyn who kept going on about the "beautiful yolk sac" she saw on the ultrasound screen.

Then, at ten weeks, we went in for a second ultrasound only to find that Yokel was dead. Where there should have been a little pulse of activity on the screen, there was nothing but a dark bleak space. According to the doctor's estimate, somewhere around eight weeks, the heart had stopped beating. For a while, it felt as though mine would, too.

Pregnancy losses really feel like a swift kick to the gut. More than that, they can throw your whole understanding of God into a tailspin. I'd always believed that God is a God who delights in birth, who loves to spread new life with a lavish hand. Why, then, did those babies die? I could understand the physical mechanics of it: an embryo caught in a fallopian tube, a fetus possibly having some defect that made it unable to survive. But that is only one very literal, basic level of comprehension. The bigger question was, If God is all-powerful, then why didn't God get in there and fix the problem? Particularly in the wake of the second loss, it was hard to feel very enthusiastic about God. Hadn't I suffered enough already? God started to feel like some grim sadist in a Quentin Tarantino film, kicking me to see how much I could take before crumpling.

Gradually, I managed to work myself out of that feeling. With the kindness of friends and family members who let me talk openly about my pain, I managed to return to my image of God as a benevolent being. Hugs helped, and so did stories of other women who had suffered pregnancy losses. What didn't help was the statement "God made this happen for a reason." That argument didn't work for me then, and it still doesn't. I just can't imagine a God who would intentionally throw some obstacle in the way of that first embryo's passage through my fallopian tube, like the little barriers of a pinball machine, leading it to a dead end. I cannot believe that God would suddenly, at eight weeks of age, stop the heartbeat of baby Yokel, this child we were so grateful to have.

And when it comes to other bad things—cancer, heart attacks, accidents, and tragic natural disasters—I don't think God makes those happen, either. It makes no logical sense or emotional sense to me that God would give us those things deliberately, knowing of the agony and pain they will bring.

Then why *do* they happen?

I have absolutely no idea.

>——<

After the miscarriage, lost in my grief, I was talking on the phone one evening to my sister Amy. She had suffered an early miscarriage between the birth of her first and second daughters, and she tried to comfort me. "When you do have a baby, and that baby arrives, you will know that this is the child you were meant to have," she said. "You will look at your baby and be totally, completely in love."

At the time, I didn't want to hear that. I did not want some hypothetical future baby. I wanted the one that was lying dead in my uterus to be resurrected, brought back to life. That was the baby I loved, already, sight unseen; that was the baby I mourned.

But I thought of my sister's words later, after Matthew's birth. He is the first baby I've ever seen who came out of the womb with his hair perfectly styled; it was literally parted neatly down the right side, slick and dark. I loved his sporty little haircut, and his little fists, and his bandy legs. And I marveled at him, at this tiny person who had been renting a space in my womb for nine months, only to come out and make his home in the world and in my arms. Two years later, there was Luke: four ounces heavier, with a prizefighter's nose and dark hair that stuck straight up in the middle, spiky-like. He looked like Matthew in some ways, but he was so clearly his own person, too. When that second child comes along, it doesn't take long to realize how unique each one is. Each of my boys has his own little expressions, his own moods, his own laugh, his own way of hugging me.

My sister was right: I can't imagine my life without either one of them. And I also know that, had those first two babies lived, I'd be saying exactly the same thing about them.

It is so tempting to wrap life up in clichés like "It was meant to be" or "This happened for a reason." But my own reproductive history has taught me that it's not quite that neat. I love Matthew and Luke with a visceral feeling that always astonishes me. I loved their tiny siblings, too. I never wanted to lose them, but I did, and now I love the ones that came after.

I am not entirely sure what the lesson is in all of this. Maybe it's that life can't be captured and summarized neatly and pithily. Maybe the lesson is that sad things still remain sad, even if there is something beautiful that would never have happened without those losses. It's tempting to leap to the ending and sum it all up with "Well, that event was sad, but something positive came out of it, so it's all good." I think the sad thing still remains sad, and it's okay to acknowledge that. It's okay to hold, in your one heart, the sadness at what you lost and the love of what you gained. And it's okay not to know why the pain happened in the first place.

More and more, as time passes, I take comfort in the words from St. Paul: "For now we see in a mirror, dimly, but then we will see face to face" (1 Corinthians 13:12). I don't have a lot of answers, and I'm wary of anyone who claims to have them all. There is some fundamental mystery at the heart of life, and I really don't think we are meant to know it, at least not yet.

In an odd way, it's comforting to realize that. It takes a lot of work to be the expert in anything, and it's sort of a relief to know that I'm not meant to have all the answers. What I am meant to do, I've come to believe, is feel my emotions as they come, discern what meaning I can, and respect the mystery. And I believe that I'm meant to hang onto what I *do* know to be true: that God is someone who loves us desperately, as I have loved all four of my children, the two whom I can hold and the two who, for reasons unknown, lost their lives while they were still inside of me, a place where I thought for sure I could have kept them safe.

In the face of all this, I also think we're called to be present to share the sorrow of others as they beat their way through their own losses. My pregnancy losses have definitely given me a kind of humility and tenderness that I didn't have before. The grief from those deaths hollowed out my insides, but in the process it uncovered the depths of my capacity to feel for others. Someone might counter with "Then that's why God gave that pain to you," but I still have a hard time accepting that theory. Maybe I'm wrong, and maybe God really did engineer those tragedies to teach me a lesson in compassion. But if he did, that compassion came at the cost of two little lives, and I just can't believe that God cooks up the world in that way. And no, I have no alternative theory as to why I lost those two babies. All I have is the belief that I should do the best I can with what I know: that God loves us and longs for us to accept that love and then spread it around, as far and wide as we can, as lavishly and as earnestly as possible.

Like my sons, I'm a child stuck on a very basic level of understanding. Right now I see as through a mirror, dimly, but someday, I'll know more. And at this moment, I'm okay with the fuzziness of it all. I am okay just sitting with the questions and opening my heart to the mystery, letting my soul prickle with the awareness of things unseen and unknown.

11

The Love of Mary

When Your Heart Leaves Your Body

When I was a kid in Catholic school, I loved Mary. She looked so pretty in her blue robes, arms outstretched, smiling serenely like a Disney princess.

But I was not a fan of pictures of Mary's Immaculate Heart. It creeped me out to see that glowing and visible heart in the center of her chest, a heart that was sometimes crowned with flame or pierced with swords. It seemed all wrong, having an internal organ like that on display for the world to see. Even when I grew into adulthood, I still found that iconography to be eerie, off-putting, and bizarre.

And then I became a mother.

When Matthew was a few weeks old, he spit up blood. It wasn't a lot of blood, just a squiggly little line on the burp cloth, but it was enough to send me spiraling into a panic. Novels in which nineteenth-century heroines cough up blood and die of tuberculosis surfaced ominously out of the depths of my memory; this is what being an English major does to you.

I called the after-hours pediatric help line and got in touch with a kind and sympathetic nurse. "Was there a lot of blood?" No, hardly any. "Does your baby seem sick?" No, he seems just fine. "I think it's probably okay," she said, "but why don't you go to the doctor in the morning just to be sure. Oh, and bring the burp cloth with you."

The next morning, Scott and I presented the pediatrician with the cloth, sealed in a Ziploc bag like forensic evidence from a crime scene. The doctor had to squint to find the miniscule line of blood, hardly visible among the pattern of bluebirds and bears and building blocks. She looked over our son thoroughly and pronounced him perfectly healthy, much to our relief.

When I called my mom and told her about the blood, she laughed somewhat wryly, which was not the reaction I expected. "You'd better get used to this, Ginny," she told me. "This is just the first of a long, long line of worries you're going to have, now that you're a parent."

And as she said that, I got a sinking feeling in my gut. I knew she was right. I would never again be completely relaxed.

Prior to Matthew's birth, I'd regarded the nine months of pregnancy as the primary minefield of my maternal life. Having lost two pregnancies already, I was terrified of losing another one, and I came to see delivery as the boundary line that would mark the Land of Obsessive Worry from the Land of Everything's Finally Okay. *If I can just get this baby out of my uterus and safely into my arms,* I thought, *I'll be in the clear.*

After Mathew's birth, I realized how spectacularly wrong I'd been. I worried that he wasn't getting enough milk to help him thrive. I obsessed about whether or not we'd installed his car seat correctly. I lived in constant fear of SIDS, that terrible angel of death that comes in the night. And as he grew out of infancy, those worries faded away, only to be replaced by others.

Now I've been at this parenting gig long enough to know that as one set of fears exits the stage, many others are lined up in the wings, waiting for their cues. And I've learned from parents of older kids that the worry never ends. You fear your child getting a driver's license, hanging out with the wrong crowd, losing her job, marrying someone who makes him miserable, struggling with infertility.

It was a few months after the birth of Matthew that I kept thinking of a well-known quotation from Elizabeth Stone, one I'd heard years before becoming a mom: "Making the decision to have a child—it is momentous. It is to decide forever to have your heart go walking around outside your body." *Bingo,* I thought as I toted Matthew around in his infant seat. That's exactly how it feels. Matthew is outside of me now, in that big scary world, and that is a very vulnerable place for a heart to be.

One day I thought back to those pictures of Mary's immaculate heart. For the first time ever, that image made perfect sense to me. Like me, Mary was a mom. Like me, she had a beloved child who was out there in the world, where any number of things could assail him. Like me, she must have felt as though the dearest, most vital part of her—her very heart—was exposed and vulnerable.

Once I made that connection, I could no longer dismiss those images as creepy and perplexing. I realized that they were, in fact, a perfect way of showing how visceral this maternal-love thing really is. It's not just something you feel in your head or in your soul. It's in your very organs, in every cell of your body, in the mechanisms that make you tick. Like any other mom, Mary felt that love, in all its exhilarating and terrifying depth.

She surely felt the fear, too, which is counterintuitive to the way we Catholics tend to think of her. It's easy to look at those serene statues and to assume that she sailed swan-like through life, calm and even, with nothing ruffling her feathers. But if you read the Gospels with a focus on what Mary was feeling during each story, it's clear that her life was anything but peaceful. As a young mother, she and her little family had to flee to a foreign country because someone wanted to kill her baby. When Jesus was a teenager, Mary and Joseph actually lost him for a few terrifying days. Then when he became an adult, he was out preaching subversive things and getting himself on the radar of powerful and merciless people who wanted nothing more than to shut him up. They did, of course, by torturing him and putting him on a cross to die—and that's the point of the story at which it's almost too hard to go on. Imagining her standing at the foot of the cross, seeing the agonizing pain and slow death of her son, is unbearable. But she stayed because it was her heart up there on that cross, and there was no way in hell she was going to leave.

As a mom, Mary took on a lot of pain. She invited vulnerability in ways that all parents do, as well as anyone who has ever loved another. I don't like that piece of it, at all. I constantly have to battle against my own worry, fighting not to let anxiety overtake me. Now that I have two children, I have twice the worry; there are two hearts trotting around outside my body. But would I change it? Absolutely not. If that's the price of love, then yes, I am willing to pay it. And there is an undeniable comfort in knowing that Mary gets it, that she had to feel the vulnerability of a mother's love.

But it's still so difficult. When Luke is jumping on our bed and falls off and whacks his head on the floor and starts to wail, my heart stops for a moment. I hold him close and tell him he'll be okay, and eventually he stops crying and squirms out of my grasp, ready to move on to the next adventure. And once my initial panic subsides, I try to learn something from his resilience and his indomitable spirit. *I'll be okay too,* I tell myself as I watch my heart run out of the room, rounding the corner and disappearing from my sight.

12

Body and Soul

This Heartburn Is for You

For all its spiritual aspects, motherhood is amazingly physical. We moms are in the business of tending to other people's little bodies, day in and day out, and our own bodies are totally involved in the process. We carry newborns in slings, so close that they feel like extensions of ourselves. We strain to grab a tissue with one hand while holding a snot-nosed child hostage with the other. Over and over we let ourselves be climbed upon and tickled and punched (playfully or otherwise). And we are capable of astonishing feats of strength, such as carrying a kicking, odiferous twenty-eight-pound toddler to the nearest airport baby-changing station (which, invariably, is halfway down the terminal). We moms submit to all of this because this is simply what we do. Motherhood is not something we can phone in. It is the very definition of *hands-on*.

For moms who physically give birth to their kids, this full-body involvement starts even earlier. With my pregnancies, wicked heartburn was always the first tip-off that something was happening down there in my uterus. Even though my ob/gyn was convinced that acid reflux didn't kick in until months later, I swear that it was always my first clue that I was in the family way. And as my pregnancies progressed, it was astonishing to see how thoroughly my body was hijacked by the demands of the very tiny person growing deep inside it. It wasn't just the weight gain or the inevitable nausea; it was also odd things I hadn't anticipated. For example, every vein on my torso became distinctly visible, as if I were a medical textbook illustration of the circulatory system. Later in the pregnancies, I'd get seriously sore legs, which Scott would uncomplainingly rub for me every evening, no doubt recognizing that he got the sweetheart deal in this whole reproductive process. And though I tried (believe me, I tried) to make him understand the full intensity of my pregnancy symptoms, I knew that he could never really get it. Is it actually possible to comprehend a physical condition that you've never experienced yourself? I think of the times other people have tried to describe an uncomfortable symptom to me, and all I can do is nod sympathetically and think, privately, that it just can't be as bad as they say. But being pregnant cured me of that reaction, if only because I understood how deeply pain can run and how it truly can incapacitate you.

What made these pregnancy symptoms worse is that I couldn't rely on my usual self-soothing strategies. Normally in stressful times, I hunker down with a steaming cup of black tea or a mug of very strong coffee tempered with half-and-half. But caffeine, like alcohol, was pretty much off the table for me; my ob/gyn was fairly conservative when it came to caffeine consumption during pregnancy. After an ectopic pregnancy and a miscarriage, I was hardly liberal myself. Then there were all those delicious foods that were suddenly *verboten*. "You can't eat soft cheese or cured meat? They didn't have those rules when I was pregnant," said my mother. This was intriguing—hey, Mom ate bacon and I turned out okay!—but again, I was disinclined to take any risks. And thanks to a particularly alarmist pregnancy guide, I began to regard artificial food coloring in the same sinister light that I'd regard anthrax. (Good-bye, gummy bears.) Then, of course, there is sex, high on everyone's list of mood lifters. Alas, after one romantic evening led to terrifying brown spotting, that particular activity was put on a long hiatus.

So basically, pregnancy was like Lent on steroids. I gave up not only candy but also coffee, coitus, and so many other things that make life pleasant. And I did it for nine months. Twice. I should have felt very holy indeed.

In an odd way, I did feel holy. It was during my pregnancy with Matthew that a certain idea clicked for me. I realized that the bodily sacrifice I was making—so many sacrifices, actually, in every aspect of my physical life—were intensely spiritual. It wasn't just that all this fasting was teaching me the art of self-denial, which nearly every religious tradition recognizes as having a spiritual benefit. For the first time ever, I was living with long-term physical discomfort, an experience that carries its own lessons. Simply put, pregnancy was the most protracted, most intense, most uncomfortable surrender of my body I had ever known.

And I hadn't even gotten to labor yet.

"You forget the pain," women used to tell me about childbirth. To this day, I can't tell you if that's true; both deliveries were C-sections. But they had their own kind of pain, and the memory of it has not faded with time. There was the laborious insertion of the IV in the back of my hand, an experience that, for a fainter like me, was pure trauma. There was the terrible moment in the OR, right after delivering Matthew, when the anesthesia lost its potency and I could actually feel the doctor pressing on my internal organs. (I've never been so glad to get laughing gas.) There was the pain in my abdomen from the C-section incision, a fiery pain that nearly made me cry every time I tried to move out of the hospital bed. Then there was trying to get the hang of nursing, which, in those early days, was anything but effortless. I had no idea that it could actually cause your breasts to bleed, or that the mere touch of a cotton nightgown against them could send you through the roof in agony. Prior to having kids, my most painful experience had been having mononucleosis in college, a sore throat that for two days straight felt like swallowing fire. But that was a day at the beach compared to the rigors of delivering my kids and learning to feed them.

And yet, because of this physical pain, I now understand something that I did not before. Call it strange, but now when I look at a crucifix, some little part of me thrums with recognition. I don't pretend to compare my own pregnancy or postpartum pains to hanging on a cross for a few hours with nails hammered through my extremities. But the central belief of the Christian faith is that Jesus gave up his own physical self, suffered in his body, so that the rest of us could have life, and life eternal. And in some very essential way, I get that now. I, too, have surrendered my body so that another person can have life. It was not easy either time; often it was deeply unpleasant, if not agonizingly painful. But both times, the experience changed me.

In her book *The Dance of the Dissident Daughter,* Sue Monk Kidd talks about how any woman who has ever breastfed has an insider's understanding of the Eucharist. I think she's right; there is something profoundly Christlike about feeding another person with your body. But for me, that awareness started earlier, during pregnancy. For nine months, a little boy was growing deep inside me, slowly being nourished by my body and blood, until he finally made a dramatic and (for me) painful exit. The entire process gives a new meaning to what Christ said at the Last Supper: "This is my body, which is given for you" (Luke 22:19). During Mass, when the priest says those words, I sometimes look at my little boys as they munch on Goldfish Crackers (my secret weapon for keeping them quiet). I love them more than I can say, those little guys. Watching them, I think: *I have given up my body, too.* And I feel lucky to have had that experience.

On the face of it, it seems odd that I see it in so positive a light. I'm no masochist; I normally make it my business to stay as far away from pain as I possibly can. And I've read enough medieval church history to know that the desire to share in Christ's suffering has, at times, resulted in some pretty bizarre behavior. But there are times when physical sacrifice does result, very directly and tangibly, in the birth or sustaining of life, and I think there is something transformative about that experience.

This is not just the province of biological mothers, by the way. People who donate blood are literally giving up their physical selves so that another person can have life. It has always struck me as a profoundly beautiful act, even though my one attempt at it ended poorly, when the nurse pricked my finger to type me and I nearly passed out ("You're not donating today," she said to my prostrate frame). And years ago, when I saw the Canadian movie *Jesus of Montreal* about actors performing a passion play, I was blown away by the ending, when the actor playing Jesus dies and his organs are donated to others in a beautiful echo of the Resurrection. Delivering and nursing a child, donating blood or bone marrow or kidneys—all these strike me as ways in which, in miniature, we can experience the physical sacrifice that lies at the heart of the Christian story. They are all ways by which the crucifix becomes subtly and powerfully more relatable—and, even more to the point, how the Resurrection does as well.

So I feel a certain kind of kinship with Jesus now. I know how it feels to surrender all physical control and to be at the mercy of forces that demand not just your time or your attention but also your very body. Twice my abdomen was cut open, in a way that seems savage and terrible (luckily, I didn't have to look). "You forget the pain," many moms say, and I think they are wrong; I have still not forgotten my own version of the pain, the terrible sting from the incision there on my abdomen, an angry line like a red and set mouth. But both times a dark-haired boy emerged from that slit in my body, purple and beautiful and squalling wildly, a new little person where formerly there was none. "It's worth it in the end," those women always used to add. About that, they are absolutely right.

13

Divine Love

An Ultrasound Picture of God

One day in fourth-grade religion class, my teacher told all of us to draw a picture of God. It stymied me as few assignments ever have. Draw God? That meant I had to know what he looked like. Correction: that meant I had to know what I *thought* he looked like, which in turn meant that I had a problem on my hands. To me, God was some faceless powerful force. I knew he was loving and forgiving, that he had made the world and everyone in it, but beyond that, I drew a pretty big blank. And even though Jesus had called God "Father," and we always prayed (at school, church, and home) using the same terminology, I never pictured God as a man, or as a woman, either. I had absolutely no visual image to offer my teacher.

But turning in a blank page was not an option for a conscientious student like me, so in the end, I dutifully took my Pentel markers and drew a man with gray hair and a gray beard. He wore a long white nightgown and had bare feet. He hovered in the air above a bed covered with a flowered bedspread, beside which a young girl with dark hair was kneeling and praying. In a speech bubble coming out of his mouth I wrote the words "My precious, precious child"—inspired, no doubt, by the "Footprints in the Sand" fable that was everywhere in the early 80s.

It was a disappointing drawing. I couldn't get God's expression right; the mouth curved down at one corner, jokily, as if God were some bad stand-up comic. And I've never been able to draw feet, so God's ended up resembling canoe oars with toes at the end. What I had tried to show as grave and serious just looked lame. I got a decent grade on the picture, but it was not an assignment that made me feel especially proud.

Even as I drew it, I knew that the entire concept of the picture was false. That wasn't my image of God, the old graybeard in the sky. Even the girl in the drawing, an obvious reference to me, was a total fabrication; I always prayed lying down in bed, never kneeling beside it. When faced with the unexplainable, I drew the accepted stereotype of God (and the accepted stereotype of prayer), all the while knowing it was totally false. It was the best I could do.

Even now, nearly thirty years later, I'd have a tough time with that assignment. It's weird to say this, but although I pray to God often, I have no firm image of whom or what I am praying to. In fact, when I try to picture God, I don't think of a person, or a face, or a body. When I think of what God looks like, I picture letters on a page: G-O-D. I'm directing my requests, my questions, and my thanks to two consonants and a vowel.

This is undeniably frustrating. With a few exceptions, I've talked to God every single day since I was six or seven; that's more than I can say about any of my other relationships. We go back pretty far, God and I, but still, he/she is maddeningly elusive. This is why I will sometimes direct my prayers to Jesus instead, mostly because he's pretty easy to picture. These days, I love the image of Christ in the framed sketch on Matthew's wall. It shows a bearded young man picking up a little boy, kissing the side of his face lovingly. It's easy to pray to the guy who enfolds you in a bear hug. Often I pray to Mary, too, who for the past ten years or so has been one of my favorite intercessors. Though I love basically every image of Mary, from the graceful white garden statues to the blonde Renaissance queens in Botticelli paintings, these days I like to think of her as a dark-haired woman, plainly dressed, with laugh lines and a somewhat weathered face. Jesus I get. Mary I get.

But God . . . well, God is like the blue shadowy outline you get when you haven't bothered to upload a profile picture to your blogger account. It's pretty strange to have someone in your life who is that elusive, someone you could never pick out of a lineup, even if your life depended on it. *What does God look like?* That mystery used to annoy me. But then I realized that I was asking the wrong question.

Every night, after bedtime, I creep into Luke's room. I take a risk and unzip the mesh tent we put on his crib when he started learning how to climb. The tearing buzz of the metal teeth usually makes him shift in his sleep, but he never wakes up. I bend down and pat his head, the fuzzy head with the very short haircut. I whisper to him as he frowns in his sleep. I touch the sharp little shoulder blades that I can feel even through his fleecy dinosaur sleeper.

Then I visit Matthew's room, tiptoeing stealthily over the hardwood floors. He lies in his toddler bed, surrounded by his stuffed animal "friends." Sometimes he's facing me, his mouth slightly open; other times, his face is to the wall. Inevitably, his hair does a wild cowlick, sticking straight up onto the pillow. I touch his head, which often feels slightly damp, as if he's just shifted from a different position on the pillow. Sometimes as I wander in he moves in his sleep, and I stop quietly, hoping not to wake him. I'm there just to see him sleep, to watch him off in dreamland, to catch those unguarded expressions that I don't see in his waking hours.

When I look at him, my heart is seized with love: it's so clear that he's growing up. The little body that used to be curled up inside my own, so long ago, is curled up on the toddler bed, which he is starting to outgrow. And that reminder of time passing just makes the love even stronger.

The first time I saw Matthew's face, it was on a grainy ultrasound photo. Scott and I waited restlessly in a small dark room while the technician prepared the images of "Bud," the baby whose gender we'd decided not to learn in advance. When Bud's picture finally came up on the screen, he was only a murky haze at first, an abstract image of splotches and light areas against a dark background. "I can never tell what I'm looking at with these ultrasound photos," Scott said, and the technician pointed it out for us. "There is the profile, with the forehead here, the mouth here, the nose here," she said, drawing with white lines on the screen as we watched, enthralled. "This is one hand, here. These five little dots are the other hand; you're seeing the fingers turned in your direction, and we're seeing just the ends of them." And then, as she explained and pointed to the screen, we could see the image suddenly resolve there before our eyes. What had been an elusive swirl of white and black was the profile of a baby: our baby. Once you saw it, you couldn't stop seeing it. The picture had cleared, and the invisible was made beautifully visible. That's Bud. That's our baby.

That night, Scott scanned in the ultrasound, and we sent it to family and friends. Since we weren't there to decipher it for them, Scott carefully drew arrows and labels on the baby's features: FORE-HEAD. RIGHT HAND. LEFT HAND. MOUTH. "Isn't that just the cutest little nose?" I gushed in the accompanying email.

And sometimes at night, when I gaze at Matthew, I remember that little nose, a tiny, turned-up curve there on the black photo. If I'm really feeling brave, I kiss it; I can't help myself. It's hard to express the intensity of love that I feel for my boys in these quiet, dimly lit moments. I love them at all times, of course, even when they are totally awake, even when they are hitting each other or refusing to eat their peas. But something about these evening vigils—watching them at their most unguarded, their most innocent, their most unaware—really grabs me right at my core. These little moments in their darkened rooms, with the shapes of stuffed animals and the train table dimly visible in the dark, are like the touchstone that reminds me, every time, of the purity of my love for them. If they have been torturing me to distraction in the hours before bedtime, these quiet moments in their sleep are the reality check. I love these little boys with more love than I would ever have imagined I'm capable of feeling. And it's a love that is actually painful sometimes. I think it's because when you care for others that intensely, that passionately, you can't help but sense the gaping hole, the bleak negative space, that would be left if they were ever gone. The possibility of loss is always there, a little nimbus hovering around the edges of even the sweetest, most crystalline moments of joy.

And it hit me recently that this is exactly how my own parents feel about me. To be honest, the first time I made that conscious connection, it rocked me back on my heels. I should clarify that in the cosmic lottery of parents, I got *way* lucky; throughout my life, my parents have always told me, "I love you," and they've always backed up that sentence with action. I've never doubted their affection, ever. But it's only lately that I've been able to internalize the type and depth of that feeling, because it's something I now feel myself. For the first time, I'm the mom who loves as well as the child who is loved. I'm both the subject and the direct object; I see the verb from both sides now. That has changed me.

And once I saw myself from my parents' perspective, a lot of things about their actions made more sense to me. All those financial sacrifices they made, everything from ballet lessons to braces to college tuition; the evenings my dad spent when I was in junior high and high school, sitting at the table, helping me with algebra or physics word problems with a practically superhuman patience while I scowled and kicked the table leg in frustration; the worries that my mom felt when I went to live abroad, a worry that she hid extremely well so as not to diminish my excitement at seeing the world; the way my dad would always check my tires before I left the house to make sure they were inflated, because I never did it myself—all of it suddenly made a whole lot more sense, on a very profound and visceral level, because that's exactly what I would do for my own boys. I got it. I get it. I really do.

And this realization leads to another epiphany, about a different parent figure. Could it also be true that God loves *me* in the same way that I love Matthew and Luke?

The only possible answer to that is yes. In fact, God probably loves me even *more* than I love them.

One thing I realized several months ago is that if we humans are making any sort of mistake in our understanding of God, it's probably that we are lowballing God's capacity for love. We take the person we adore most in the world, and we decide that that is how God loves us. That estimate is probably the best we can do, but the thing is, even that kind of human love has to be short of the mark. How can we, with our limited understanding, ever be *over*estimating the endless goodness and warmth that are God? I don't think it's possible. I simply can't believe that we are going to die and end up face-to-face with God, only to hear God say, "You know what?

You gave me too much credit. I *don't* really love you as much as you thought I did." God is not the fickle friend you had when you were twelve, who after months of eating lunch with you at school suddenly decides not to invite you to her birthday party. God is more like the mom who lets you cry on her lap and listens and gives you endless hugs and tells you that you're special and who slowly, through that immense love, rehabilitates your image of yourself and the world. With that love, you can go on. You can even, maybe, find yourself forgiving the perfidious friend. That is the power of a parent's love. And it's why being a mom is probably the closest that I will come toward understanding how much God loves me. It's not the whole picture, but I think it's the best I'll be able to do here on earth.

And we parents do so many things for our kids, things that simply don't make sense without some larger purpose. On any given day, I help construct train layouts, open juice boxes, administer hugs, answer the innumerable string of whys, laugh at toddler knock-knock jokes, and feign interest in the fact that there is a taxi in the next lane. Many of these things I do because I love my boys and for no other reason. It may occur to Matthew, sometime when he's an adult, that maybe Mom didn't really enjoy reading that favorite book about vehicles that had about eighty-six flaps to open. And he may realize that my willingness to sit and look at it with him was an expression of pure, complete love. Because I'm realizing that parenting is sort of like God's creation of this world: it doesn't really make sense if there isn't a fathomless, ceiling-less, limitless love behind it all. Even my own little nighttime forays into the boys' rooms, watching them as they sleep, is a habit that would have sounded creepy to me at some pre-parent point in my life. But I do it because of the love I have for them, a love that can't keep me away.

That's a pretty heady realization.

Not all of my questions about God have been answered, not by a long shot. There's much that I don't understand, that I probably won't figure out this side of the grave. And when I pray, I still find myself picturing three letters, G-O-D, rather than an actual being. But I'm okay with this. Having a visual image of God seems less important than it used to.

Because I've realized that if I could do that fourth-grade assignment all over again, I wouldn't flail like I did before. This time, I'd take an entirely different approach. Rather than drawing God, I'd draw a picture of the world as I think God sees it. I'd sketch a small boy in a little bed, curled up in sleep, the object of a love that can never fully be put into words. That little boy doesn't know it, but he's given me something that is utterly beyond price. Just as the ultrasound technician pointed out Matthew's fingers and nose, so my sons have pointed me toward a truth that was once vague and elusive. As I kiss my sleeping boys, I'm seeing something about God that I couldn't find by myself. The image has cleared, and the invisible has become visible. It isn't the whole picture, but it's enough.

14

Heaven

Playing Go Fish in Paradise

When I was a kid, the cartoons and comic strips were pretty clear about what heaven looked like. It was a place in the sky where people floated around in halos and long white robes. There were clouds and only clouds as far as the eye could see, and there seemed to be little to do there other than playing the harp.

As an adult, it's pretty easy to dismiss this idea of heaven as a cloud-filled lounge in the sky. It's much harder to come up with an alternative vision. In *Hamlet,* Shakespeare describes the afterlife as "the undiscovered country, from whose bourn / No traveler returns," as if to imply that death is like flying to another country and then being stranded there because of eternal airline strikes. This description rings true to me. How can those of us down here really know what it's like on the other side of the border? Who can come back and tell us?

I do believe in heaven, and I hope to get there someday. I have found comfort over the years in picturing loved ones such as my grandparents alive for all eternity; it has mitigated the sting of losing them. But when it comes to imagining the specifics—What exactly do you do there? Do you get to hang out with people you knew in life? Do you miss the people you left behind on earth?—I've spent very little time or energy worrying about the answers. Until recently.

For ten years, I had a very good friend named Mary. It feels surreal and awful to write "had," but Mary died last year, two days before her forty-eighth birthday. She was the kind of person for whom positive adjectives just spill out of my pen: fun-loving, adventurous, creative, spiritual, empathetic, loyal, thoughtful, courageous. She drew on that courage during two separate bouts of cancer. The first, uterine cancer, rocked her world when she was only thirty-four. The doctors gave her a twenty-percent chance of surviving, but she defied the odds, and three years after that, I was introduced to her at a party in her apartment. She and my husband had been friends for years, and a few weeks after Scott and I started dating, I found myself sitting in Mary's living room, looking at this cancer survivor with the light brown hair and trendy glasses and vibrant energy. Welcoming as she was, it was clear that she was also making sure I was good enough for Scott, who had been a huge support to her throughout her terrifying diagnosis, treatment, and recovery.

"The truth is," she told me, with the straight-from-the-heart directness that I came to know as one of her hallmarks, "Scott is one of the very best people I've ever known."

"I know what you mean," I said. "It didn't take me long to figure that out."

Mary's eyes filled with tears, and from that moment on, we were friends.

Over the next ten years, she became one of the people I trusted most. Mary had the ability to make friends everywhere she went. When you talked, she was utterly present. The suffering she'd experienced had intensified her natural, instinctive empathy, and she was the perfect person to call when you were going through a hard time. She did not minimize your pain or offer platitudes. She felt your pain and sat in the middle of it with you and somehow said just the right thing.

Mary's gifts found an outlet in her work as an elementary school teacher, working in a low-income community. She adored the students she taught, many of them immigrants, some of them in the country illegally. When there were ICE (Immigration and Customs Enforcement) raids in her community, she suffered with the children who lived in fear of a knock on the door. She saw the beauty and intelligence and promise in her kids, and she shared it with anyone who would listen—most important, with the kids themselves. Her love of Latin American culture was evident in her devotion to Our Lady of Guadalupe, the patron saint of Mexico. In Mary's house you could see Our Lady everywhere: in icons, framed pictures, magnets, and painted on a folk-art cabinet. Mary once told me how she disliked the classical images of the Virgin Mary that were pale white, which made her "the translucent-looking lady." The earth tones of Our Lady of Guadalupe's skin were, to her, far more beautiful.

Mary also believed in a God who was pure love and who would never exclude anyone. When she married Tom, the wedding Mass included a prayer that lesbian, gay, and transgender Catholics would always feel welcome in the church. It was quintessentially Mary, noticing and feeling compassion for those on the margins.

"I've learned so much from your spirituality," I told her once, standing in the parking lot of the church. "You include everyone, without exception, and you reach out to people on the outside. I find that so inspiring."

She shrugged off my compliment. "I just don't understand why everybody doesn't do that," she said. "I mean, that's what this faith is all about. That's the whole *point*."

Mary found beauty in everyone and everything, even the most unlikely places. She was a gifted photographer who could see the graceful angles in a pair of weather-beaten old doors, or the vivid splash of color in a bin of erasers in a store. Long before it became fashionable to do so, she was taking artistic photos of her pregnant friends, their bellies on full display. She'd scout locations—from a sun-warmed grassy hillside to the big blue wall in the IKEA parking lot—and let the mom-to-be decide how much of herself she wanted to show. Many of Mary's friends have hilarious stories of being partially or completely naked and diving into bushes or behind boulders, waiting for pedestrians to pass by so that the session could continue. I don't know whether it was sheer luck or divine intervention, but no one ever got arrested for indecent exposure. From Mary's artistic perspective, it was worth flirting with danger to get the perfect shot. And there was an added poignancy to this hobby because Mary herself could never have children; the cancer had robbed her of her uterus. Though she wasn't a mother herself, she was a godmother to many children, including Matthew. One of her older godchildren had christened her "GodMary," and that's how she became known to Matthew and Luke, who adored her. She had an irrepressible sense of fun and a true respect for young kids. They knew they were safe with her.

That was Mary: artistic, outgoing, hilarious, generous, loving. She had beaten back cancer once, and for twelve years, it stayed away. But then she began to experience symptoms of jaundice. She developed odd blisters on her skin, which looked almost like chicken pox but were actually a sign that something was wrong with her liver. The blisters were terribly itchy, and she could not stop scratching. For a while the doctors thought it was something else, but then it became clear: it was cancer, taking up residence in a new part of her body.

It was hard to believe and hard to face. A few months after her symptoms started, the surgeons opened her up and realized that the cancer was so widespread that it was impossible to remove it; they simply closed her up. The best-case scenario was that she had two years to live; the worst-case scenario was that she had two months. It was all so terrible that I refused to believe it. I knew she had beaten the odds years earlier, and I knew that she was a fighter. I kept praying, and I desperately held on to faith that something would happen, that she'd be okay.

But shortly after the surgery, when Scott and I left the boys with my mom and drove up to Mary's house to visit, she was weak and tired and more depressed than I'd ever seen her. She wrapped herself in a quilt, and we sat and talked in the living room, surrounded by images of Our Lady of Guadalupe, the profile of mountains outside the window. Mary talked about death, about heaven, and she struggled to wrap her head around it. "I don't get it," she said. "What do you do in heaven? I know there are supposed to be angels and saints and all, but really, what do you do there? Are you still yourself? Do you just sit around for all eternity?" She feared that she would be bored there—and the more I thought about her questions, the more I realized that they made sense. Just sitting around for an eternity seems tremendously dull.

Scott, with his background in theology, talked about the Catholic understanding of heaven as a place where you join the others who have died before you, and where you take an active interest in what happens on earth. "Catholics have traditionally believed that when you're there, you're not cut off from the world," he said. "You are actively involved. You pray for the people you knew and cared about when you were alive. You continue to do things on their behalf."

Mary asked a lot of questions that day. She talked about how weary she felt at the prospect of another round of cancer, this kind even more insidious and painful than the last. At one point, in a moment of stark honesty, she said, "I sort of feel like it might be better if a huge truck hit me tomorrow and I just died all at once."

I grabbed her hand. "Look," I told her, "we want you to stay as long as you can. We want every second of Mary time that we can possibly get."

She started to cry. "That's what I needed to hear," she said. "I know that's true, deep inside, but somehow, I still need to hear people say it to me."

Over the next few months, Mary's condition went up and down. She'd get fevers, dangerous ones, which required trips to the ER and often resulted in hospitalization. Once she contracted sepsis in the hospital and nearly died. We were all grateful that she and Tom were able to join us on our annual group camping trip, a fun time together on San Pablo Bay. And though I knew that Mary's situation was critical, my denial continued. There are some things you simply refuse to face. It seemed impossible that Mary, one of the most alive and vibrantly creative people I knew, was edging close to death, to crossing that line from which no traveler returns.

And hovering in the back of my mind was the thought of what would happen if she did die; we would have to tell our boys. I had worked so hard to keep scary, awful things out of their little world. How would they handle this? I worried especially about Matthew, Mary's godson, who was five. And because the thought of introducing death into his little world was so horrible to face, it was easier to roll that into the overall sense of denial.

One Sunday, we were planning to join Mary and Tom for dinner at the home of a mutual friend, when Luke threw up. Not wanting to expose Mary to his germs, I stayed home with him while Matthew and Scott went to dinner. During the evening, I called to say hi. Mary got on the phone, and we talked for about forty-five minutes. I asked how she was doing, hoping for specifics, and her answers, couched in a kind of careful avoidance, indicated that things were not good. Then we chatted about this and that, with the occasional sound in the background of children laughing and shrieking, running through the room where Mary sat with the phone. In general, her spirits were good. But she grew serious toward the end of our conversation and spoke of something that was weighing on her. "I just don't want to go without being able to tell everybody how much I love them."

I told her that she didn't need to worry. We knew. Mary was never one to hide her affection.

"I just want you to know," she said, "how much you Moyers have meant to me."

When the conversation was over, I hung up the phone and went into the kitchen and cried. Because I knew then, in a way I could no longer deny, that she was dying.

Mary became progressively more frail and thin. Her round face began to shrivel. It was as if the cancer was whittling her out, leaving a kind of shell of the body she used to inhabit. She was in great discomfort a lot of the time, and she vomited often and could not eat much because even a small amount of food made her feel very full.

I saw her for the last time on a Saturday in November. I had joined three other friends in Mary's home; we were there to see her and to take care of any tasks around the house she wanted us to do. Her request was that we work in the garden, so, armed with shears and rakes and shovels, we trimmed the roses and weeded and removed an old dead plant with tenacious roots. (We pretended it was Mary's cancer, and it gave us great satisfaction to yank it out.) Mary was yellow from the jaundice, as if her skin had been colored over with a highlighter pen. She wore a bright orange T-shirt with a jack-o'-lantern face on it—a typically whimsical Mary gesture, which also seemed, somehow, that she was giving the jaundice the bird. ("You think you can make me glow? I'll show you a color that *really* glows!") We tried to get her to sit down and simply direct us, but she insisted on helping, clipping back a hydrangea bush and doing whatever she could until she had to stop and catch her breath or vomit.

I know now how graced those moments were. Four friends in a garden, the scent of lavender and damp soil around us, as we cleaned up Mary's little patch of earth. But it was terribly painful, too.

As I squinted at the gravel path, determined not to let a single miniscule weed escape my notice, Mary talked to us again about heaven. She had heard that some people believe that when you die, you become just like a drop in the ocean. She found that image very distressing. I didn't pry, but I think that idea scared her because it seemed like disappearing, like being subsumed. And when she had lost so much already—her health, her ability to work, her hope for a joyful future—it seemed too awful to think of losing her very identity as well.

Our priest, Father Xavier, had been by the house to visit her earlier that week, and she told us of their conversation. She had pressed him to tell her what heaven would be like. She wanted to know. As she neared the end, I think she needed to know.

"Mary," he had said, "I honestly don't know what heaven is going to be like. But I do know this: it has to be way better than we could ever imagine."

>———<

A few weeks later, on December 12, the feast day of Our Lady of Guadalupe, I was sitting in my classroom around noon, and I checked my phone. There was a message from Scott saying that Mary had died earlier that morning.

As I sat at my desk and cried, I thought about how at that very moment, Mary was somewhere else. Her questions about the afterlife had been answered; her struggle with them was over. She had passed through to the other side, and she knew it all now. She had the knowledge that she had wanted for months. And for a moment, that gave me peace.

I tried to hang on to that peace later, as I thought of breaking the news to Matthew. Scott and I decided we'd talk to him that evening, when we could both be there, so the rest of the afternoon was a waiting game. When I got home from school, I tried to compose myself and save my tears for the boys' rest period, when Matthew would be reading quietly in his room. But it felt awful, like possessing some explosive knowledge that could smash his happy innocence to smithereens. I passed by his room at one point and looked in, and he was sitting on his bed, reading a story out of his Curious George Treasury, patiently sounding out the words and using a huge green magnifying glass to make them larger. It was the book Mary had given him for his third birthday, and as I looked at him, so sweet and innocent, I felt my heart break along a new fracture line.

He turned and saw me in the doorway and smiled broadly and waved. I smiled back.

Later that evening, after Luke was down in bed and the dinner dishes were put away, Scott and I invited Matthew to sit on the couch with us. We had to pry him away from his current pursuit: photographing Christmas tree ornaments with our old camera, a pastime that refreshed my grief with thoughts of Mary and her favorite hobby.

We settled him on the sofa between us. "Matthew," Scott said gently, "do you know how GodMary has been sick lately?"

He nodded.

"Well," Scott continued after a pause, "she died this morning."

Matthew looked up swiftly. "She died?"

"Yes."

He looked down, frowning slightly, and it was as if I could see the wheels in his mind turning, processing what it all meant.

"Her body got so sick that it broke," I told him. "The doctors couldn't fix it. They tried very hard, but they couldn't fix it." He was quiet and it killed me, looking at his little face, his bent head, and wondering what parts of his world this was rocking and how his brain was having to stretch in a new direction to process this information.

"This means we can't see her anymore," I said.

"We can't?"

"No. But we can still talk to her. We can pray to her, because she's in heaven now, with Jesus, and that is a good place to be."

He couldn't even get to heaven yet. "Where did she die?"

"At home, honey."

There was a pause. Then he asked, "Who will be with God-Tom now?"

The next morning, as Scott drove Matthew to preschool, the questions continued. Matthew wanted to know more about the doctors and how they tried to help her. He wanted to know how we would be able to talk to her, now that she was no longer alive, answers that Scott fielded as best he could. And that was how it went, for a few days: no noisy tears, for which I was somewhat relieved, but the occasional question.

He was processing it, trying to make sense of it all. As was I, in fact.

In the weeks that followed, we helped plan a rosary and funeral. We attended a celebration of life in her hometown in central California. There was such a comfort in meeting with other people who loved her, who were feeling what we were feeling.

Over the weeks, memories of Mary kept drifting back to me, little rafts bringing both pain and comfort. I remembered how Mary and Tom always used to come to our house on New Year's Eve for games and wine and Dick Clark, and then they'd stay overnight. That last New Year's, Mary itched terribly from the blisters, especially on her feet, and the itching grew unbearable at night. The only way she could go to sleep was to put ice on her feet; she brought along her own ice packs and stowed them in our freezer, ready for use after midnight. I tried to comprehend a reality in which sleeping with frozen feet was preferable to the alternative.

But in spite of that, we had a good New Year's, playing games and getting hilarious texts from Tom, who was doing sound engineering for the local Grateful Dead concert and couldn't join us. The next morning Mary admitted that she had had a pretty sleepless night—typical, given her symptoms—but she rallied, playing with the boys and settling in with a cup of coffee. I went for a walk after breakfast and came back to find Mary sitting on the floor by the coffee table, ensconced in a game of Go Fish with Matthew and Scott. Matthew had gotten the game for Christmas, and not being thrilled about the idea of spending half an hour with a fan of penguin-shaped cards, I'd been putting off his requests to play. But Mary was camped out happily on the floor, sitting down at Matthew's level and teaching him the game. Matthew was thrilled to be the focus of her attention. It was obvious that Mary was loving it, too, even though she had to stop every few seconds to scratch her feet.

Somehow, that image kept coming back to me when I thought of Mary and of her relationship with Matthew. Sometimes, when you are beleaguered by the daily demands of parenting, you need someone else to show you how fun it can be to spend time with your own kids.

Months passed. When we tucked Matthew in at night, we continued to pray for Mary just as we had during her illness. I knew that those prayers weren't required anymore; as one of my friends said, Mary is now the one praying for us. But Scott and I admitted to each other that eliminating her from our prayers felt too awful and final. We kept it up.

And occasionally, Matthew would bring her up in conversation. One evening, during dinner, I looked at the flowers in the vase on the table: old shriveled daffodils, starting to curl around the edges. "I guess I'd better throw these flowers away," I said, "because they're dead."

Matthew said, "I don't like the word *dead*. It makes me sad."

"Why is that?"

"Because it makes me think of GodMary."

I had to take a moment to collect myself before answering. "It makes me sad when I think of GodMary, too."

"Why?"

"Because I loved her, and she's not here anymore. And I wish I could see her again."

There was a pause. Then Matthew asked the kind of question that makes perfect sense, coming from a five-year-old boy. "Will scientists dig her fossils out of the earth?"

If Mary had been there, her laughter would have ricocheted around the room. I would give so much to be able to hear that laugh again.

Grief, as a good friend once told me, isn't linear. It's not like you get a little better every day. Some days you're fine; other days, something happens to make you feel like a ball in a pinball machine, pinging crazily up and down from happiness to pain. And eight months later, there are times when the grief at losing Mary feels totally raw and new.

And through all of this, through all of Mary's questions about death and Matthew's questions about death, I've had to think about it in a way I never have before. I'm so poorly equipped to say for sure what the afterlife is like. The only thing I can say with certainty is that when you're in heaven, you're with Jesus, and that has to be as good as it gets.

And, like Mary, I resist the notion that you lose your uniqueness in the afterlife. Mary shared so much of herself with others when she was alive; I don't think death could stop her singular generosity of spirit. As I've worked on this book, in fact, I've asked her to pray for me and my writing, because she always cared about it and understood the creative life. I believe that she still loves me as I still love her. I feel her supporting all of us, praying for her godson Matthew and her other godchildren and the rest of us Moyers and her family and friends and students and all those who feel marginalized by society, just as she did in life. A love like Mary's doesn't die, and a personality like Mary's lives on. I'm convinced of that.

And somehow, when I think of what she's doing now, I have this image of her sitting on the floor with a bunch of children, a sheaf of Go Fish cards in her hand. There must be lots of kids in heaven, kids whose moms aren't there yet, and I like to think that Mary is teaching them all how to play. Her feet aren't itching, and her body is beautifully restored. She's laughing and happy, and she's not bored at all.

Epilogue

God in the Bubbles

When Luke was two, we went through a period when Sunday Mass posed a unique challenge. He'd be okay for a time, prowling around the pew and munching on Goldfish Crackers, but then he'd catch a whiff of freedom and make a run for it. You can get only so much from a homily when you are sprinting after a toddler who is hell-bent on making it to the vestibule before being tackled. It was less like Sunday Mass and more like a football game, one in which you are painfully aware that the other player is in way better shape than you are.

So one Sunday morning, we decided not to fight it anymore. Scott took Matthew off to Mass, and I stayed home with my little athlete.

I was sorry to miss Mass, because I really like going. It's a way to bookend my week with ritual, to feel a part of something larger than myself and my own small worries. And I am always better off for having the body of Christ within me.

But once I got over the oddness of being home instead of at Mass, I started to enjoy it. For one thing, it was a freakishly warm day for February, the kind of winter's day you sometimes get in northern

California. Taking advantage of the sun, I took Luke outside to blow bubbles. We sat out on the front walkway with our little plastic jars. The street was quiet, the only sound coming from a few birds as they chirped and fluttered their wings inside a curtain of jasmine. My daffodils were just beginning to bloom, little sunbursts in the bare brown beds.

Luke reached inside the bubble bottle for the wand, and I sat near him, the cement cool and rough underneath me, the sun intoxicatingly warm. Every now and then I reached to help him, but he was intent on doing it himself, pudgy little fingers grabbing the wrong end of the wand and holding it up, trying to blow from too far away. His concentration was astonishing: even when the wand slipped far down inside the bubble solution, he kept reaching for it, without frustration, peering curiously into the bottle. It always amazes me, that strong focus he has, that ability to throw himself totally into a problem without complaining. Sometimes it can be challenging, like when he's concentrating on a task and won't be diverted for dinner or bath. Most of the time, though, it's a trait I admire. I figure I can learn a lot from it.

Once we had recovered the wand, I leaned toward it and blew gently. A few bubbles sailed off into the lawn. Luke smiled, that secret little smile that makes my heart ache, and I rubbed his shoulders underneath his orange shirt.

And I realized, as we sat basking in the sun, that I was perfectly happy. There was a sudden sense of well-being and peace, the kind I used to get in deep prayer: the feeling that you are totally in the moment and the moment is good. It is the sense that, for a beautiful space of time, you are exactly where God wants you to be, doing exactly what God made you to do.

Some of us experience that feeling on a retreat or in a church on Sunday morning, and those are natural places to look for it. But

I've learned that you can also find it in the front yard, with viscous bubble soap pooled on the cement beside you and birdsong in the air. You can find it in the gift of a spontaneous morning playdate, a golden sliver of time that you didn't plan in advance. Most of all, you can find it in the presence of the sweet small person next to you, who teaches you more than you ever thought you'd know about patience and purpose and peace.

When we were done, we put the cap back on the bubbles, got off the concrete, and went inside. It was one little moment of motherhood, here and then gone. I still remember it vividly, though, because it's a perfect example of what I've learned from this wild ride called parenting: Grace shows up everywhere, in random places and at random moments. And if you savor those moments—if you let yourself inhabit them fully, if you fix them in your heart, if you recognize the touch of God in them—then you realize that they aren't so random after all. Taken all together, they are like the individual brushstrokes that make up an Impressionist painting. They reveal the picture of a life that is colorful and sometimes chaotic, yes. But it's bathed in light, and more meaningful than you ever imagined a life could be.

Acknowledgments

To Joe Durepos: Thank you for liking what you saw and for helping to make this book a reality. I'm profoundly grateful for your vision (and your patience!). Thank you to Vinita Hampton Wright for the perceptive editing and to Andrew Yankech for the enthusiastic marketing. Thanks also to Steve Connor and to the Loyola design team for the gorgeous cover.

I'm so grateful for the family and friends who kept asking, over the space of a few years, how my next book was coming along. Your interest and support mean more than I can say. A special shout-out to Tarn Wilson and to Lisa Hillhouse for your advice and enthusiasm.

To Mom and Dad: You always made parenting look so easy (even though I know now that it wasn't). Thanks for your love, and for giving me the gift of a happy childhood. To Amy: having an older sister means someone always blazes the path for you. Thanks for showing me how fulfilling motherhood could be.

To Mary Donovan-Kansora: your time on this earth was way too short, but I am so grateful that I got to share it with you. We once talked about how grief is the price we pay for love. You said that love was worth it. It is.

To Matthew and Luke, my muses in footed pajamas: whenever I forget, you remind me about what really matters. I love you forever and ever.

Most of all, to Scott: you're my rock, my sounding board, my staunch advocate, my seatmate on this crazy roller coaster ride. Thank you for believing in this book and for believing in me. I love you. P.S. God is smiling.

About the Author

Ginny Kubitz Moyer is a contributor to several print and online publications, including *U.S. Catholic* magazine, BustedHalo.com, and CatholicMom.com. Her book, *Mary and Me,* is a Catholic Press Award winner. She and her husband live in the San Francisco Bay area with their two sons. She blogs at RandomActsOfMomness.com.

Also Available

Thrift Store Saints
Meeting Jesus 25¢ at a Time
$13.95 • Pb • 3301-2

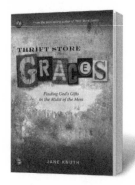

Thrift Store Graces
Finding God's Gifts in the Midst of the Mess
$13.95 • Pb • 3692-1

Small Mercies
Glimpses of God in Everyday Life
$12.95 • Pb • 3695-2

Recipe for Joy
A Stepmom's Story of Finding Faith, Following Love, and Feeding a Family
$13.95 • Pb • 3795-9

To order: call 800-621-1008,
visit www.loyolapress.com/store,
or visit your local bookseller.

Continue the Conversation

If you enjoyed this book, then connect with Loyola Press to continue the conversation, engage with other readers, and find out about new and upcoming books from your favorite spiritual writers.

Visit us at
www.LoyolaPress.com
to create an account
and register for our
newsletters.

Or you can just click on the code to the right with your smartphone to sign up.

Connect with us on the following:

Facebook   **Twitter**   **You Tube**
facebook.com/loyolapress   twitter.com/loyolapress   youtube.com/loyolapress